Thomas Alva Edison

Inventing the Electric Age

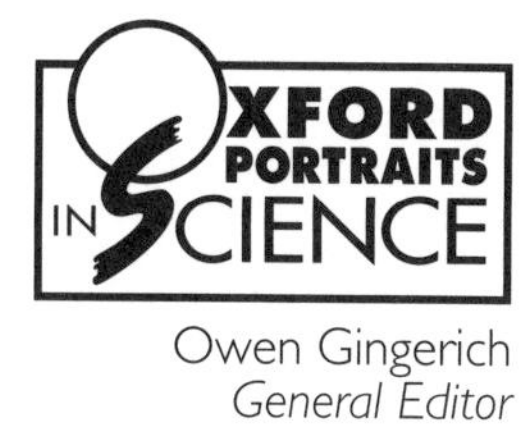

Owen Gingerich
General Editor

Thomas Alva Edison

Inventing the Electric Age

Gene Adair

Oxford University Press
New York • Oxford

To Leslie

Oxford University Press

Oxford New York
Athens Auckland Bangkok Bogotá Bombay
Buenos Aires Calcutta Cape Town Dar es Salaam
Delhi Florence Hong Kong Istanbul Karachi
Kuala Lumpur Madras Madrid Melbourne
Mexico City Nairobi Paris Singapore
Taipei Tokyo Toronto Warsaw
and associated companies in
Berlin Ibadan

First published in 1996 by Oxford University Press, Inc.,
198 Madison Avenue, New York, New York 10016
First issued as an Oxford University Press paperback in 1997

Design: Design Oasis
Layout: Leonard Levitsky
Picture research: Lisa Kirchner

Library of Congress Cataloging-in-Publication Data
Adair, Gene.
Thomas Alva Edison / Gene Adair.
P. cm. — (Oxford Portraits in Science)
Includes bibliographical references and index.
ISBN 0-19-508799-2 (library edition)
ISBN 0-19-511981-9 (paperback)
1. Edison, Thomas A. (Thomas Alva), 1847–1931—Juvenile literature.
2. Inventors—United States—Biography—Juvenile literature.
3. Electric engineers—United States—Biography—Juvenile literature.
[1. Edison, Thomas A. (Thomas Alva), 1847–1931. 2. Inventors.]
I. Title. II. Series.
TK140.E3A62 1996
621.3'092—dc20 95-37499
CIP

9 8 7 6

Printed in the United States of America
on acid-free paper

Frontispiece: *Edison at work in the chemical department of his West Orange laboratory about 1890.*

Contents

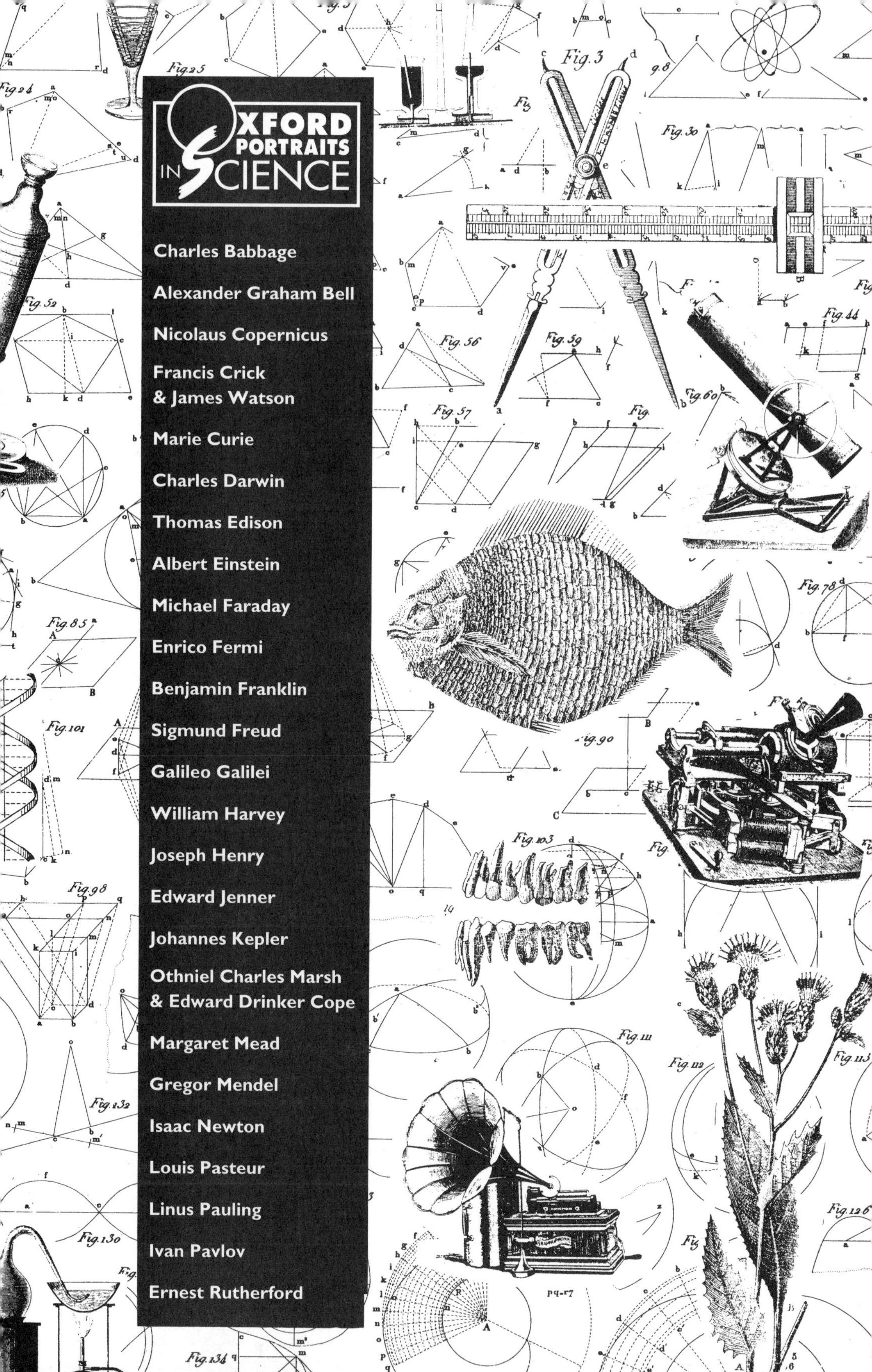
OXFORD PORTRAITS IN SCIENCE
Charles Babbage
Alexander Graham Bell
Nicolaus Copernicus
Francis Crick
& James Watson
Marie Curie
Charles Darwin
Thomas Edison
Albert Einstein
Michael Faraday
Enrico Fermi
Benjamin Franklin
Sigmund Freud
Galileo Galilei
William Harvey
Joseph Henry
Edward Jenner
Johannes Kepler
Othniel Charles Marsh
& Edward Drinker Cope
Margaret Mead
Gregor Mendel
Isaac Newton
Louis Pasteur
Linus Pauling
Ivan Pavlov
Ernest Rutherford

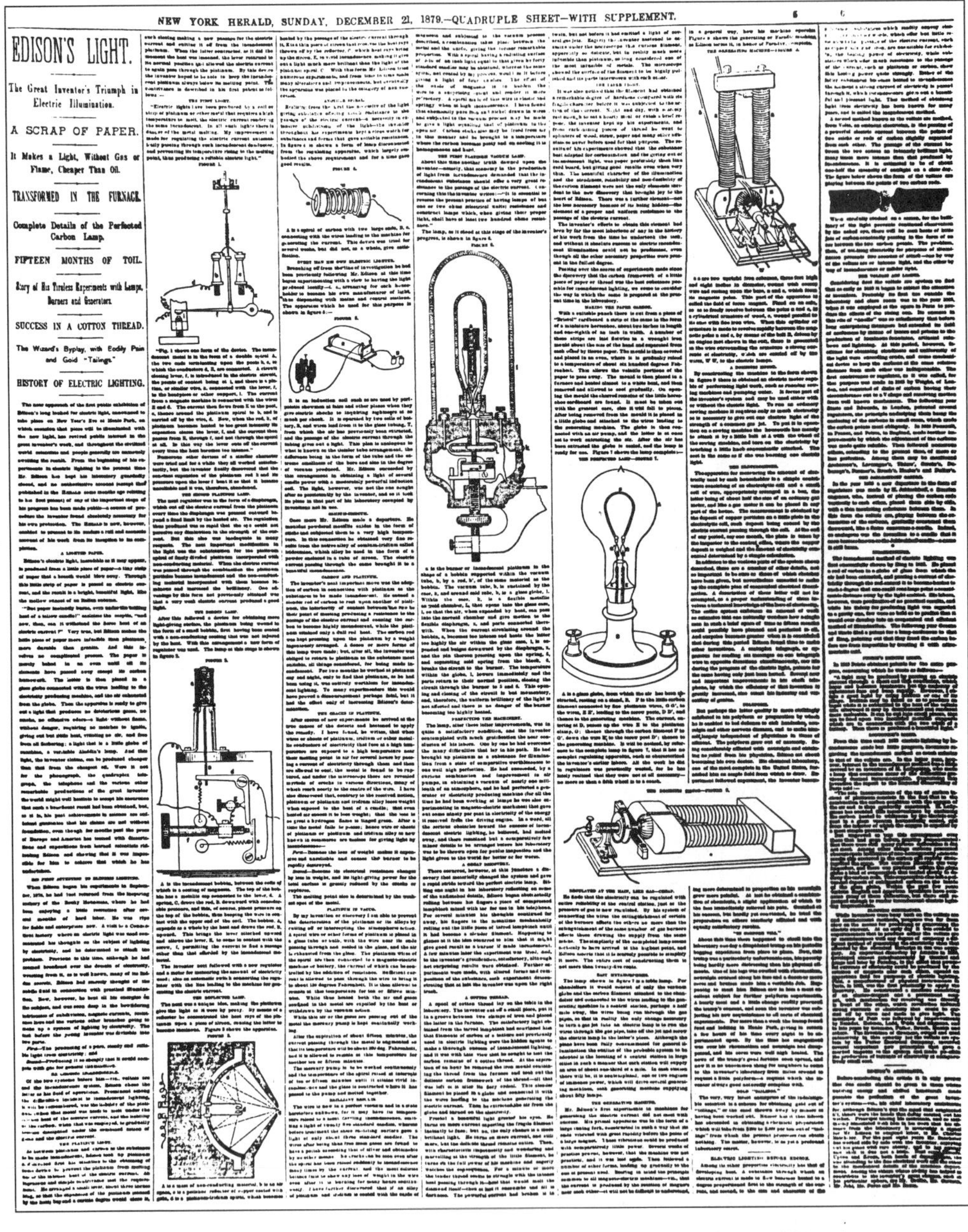

NEW YORK HERALD, SUNDAY, DECEMBER 21, 1879.—QUADRUPLE SHEET—WITH SUPPLEMENT.

EDISON'S LIGHT.

The Great Inventor's Triumph in Electric Illumination.

A SCRAP OF PAPER.

It Makes a Light, Without Gas or Flame, Cheaper Than Oil.

TRANSFORMED IN THE FURNACE.

Complete Details of the Perfected Carbon Lamp.

FIFTEEN MONTHS OF TOIL.

Story of His Tireless Experiments with Lamps, Burners and Generators.

SUCCESS IN A COTTON THREAD.

The Wizard's Byplay, with Bodily Pain and Gold "Tailings."

HISTORY OF ELECTRIC LIGHTING.

On December 21, 1879, the New York Herald *dedicated an entire page to the astonishing news of Edison's success with gasless lighting. A public demonstration of the lighting system took place on New Year's Eve, 10 days later.*

A Festival of Light

On the evening of December 31, 1879, the tiny village of Menlo Park, New Jersey, became the site of a New Year's party unlike any the world had ever seen. People were arriving by the trainload to gaze in awe at the latest wonder to emerge from the laboratory of the inventor Thomas Alva Edison.

Just two years before, Edison had astounded the world with the phonograph—a machine that talked. To the crowds that were swarming to Menlo Park that evening, he had promised something even more amazing. It was an electric light that could be used in homes, offices, and schools—a remarkable technical innovation that promised to make gas lighting and oil lamps obsolete. The product of months of intensive labor, the invention was now ready for display to the general public.

As the visitors arrived at the little Menlo Park station, they were greeted with a series of glowing glass bulbs mounted on posts along the street leading toward Edison's laboratory. Bulbs burned as well in six nearby houses. Two lights shone above the gate at the entrance to the laboratory grounds, while several more illuminated the yard surrounding the lab.

Entering the laboratory—a two-story building 100 feet long and 30 feet wide—the visitors found its rooms aglow with 25 more bulbs. Shining softly and steadily, without the familiar flicker of gaslight, the lights were easy on the eyes.

"There's Edison!" someone cried, and dozens of heads turned to catch a glimpse of the inventor. Most were probably surprised to see how young he was—not quite 33 years old. And with his ill-cropped brown hair and chemical-stained clothes, a handkerchief knotted at his neck instead of a tie, he was clearly not one who put on airs. Instead, he gave the impression of a man too driven by his work to care about his physical appearance.

In the plain speech of his midwestern background, Edison explained how the marvelous light worked. An electric generator supplied power to the lamps. Inside each of the glass bulbs, from which the air had been evacuated, the electric current flowed through a thin, horseshoe-shaped filament of carbon, causing it to glow.

"How you got the red-hot hairpin into that bottle?" one man asked. Others wanted to know how much the lamps cost and how efficiently they operated.

After many months of frustrating experimentation, Edison finally found the perfect material for the filament of his electric lamp—carbon.

Edison and his assistants gave several demonstrations. They submerged one of the lamps in a jar filled with water; they kept it there for four hours and it burned steadily the entire time. To imitate the heavy use that a lamp might receive in the average household, they rapidly switched one of them on and off—with no adverse effects on the lamp's performance. The inventor also demonstrated an electric motor, using it to run a sewing machine and a water pump. He thus showed the crowd that electricity was good for things other than lighting lamps.

A few minor incidents enlivened the evening. A woman who got too close to one of the generators discovered the power of its magnetic field when her hairpins suddenly flew off her head. A rival inventor, clearly drunk, loudly proclaimed that it was all a trick; the crowd told him to shut up. There was even a would-be saboteur present. An employee of one of the gaslight companies—the industry that had the most to lose if Edison's invention proved a success—tried to use a concealed wire to short-circuit the lamps. When the safety fuses that had been installed in the system kept him from doing any real damage, Edison's men nabbed him and escorted him to the door.

By the time the public exhibition was over, more than 3,000 people had flowed through the doors of Edison's laboratory. They had traveled from New York City, Trenton, Philadelphia, and many points in between. They returned to their homes knowing that they had witnessed something historic.

And yet, what they had seen that New Year's Eve in Menlo Park was only a hint of what was to come. Edison envisioned a system of electrical distribution that could light entire cities. Within a few decades, that dream would be a reality throughout the world.

Edison's system of light and power was arguably the greatest of his accomplishments. Yet, impressive as this achievement was, it represented only a fraction of his work. In a career that lasted more than 60 years, he received nearly 1,100 patents—more than any other inventor—for innovations large and small. He played a critical role in the improvement of both the telegraph and telephone, and in addition to the electric power industry, he launched two others: sound recording and motion pictures. His impact on the quality of modern life has been immeasurable.

Edison became a folk hero during his own lifetime and remains one to this day. A large part of his appeal lay in the fact that he was a self-made man. Americans seem to reserve a special affection for those who spring from humble beginnings, acquire their learning as best they can, and go on to great accomplishments. Edison fit the pattern well.

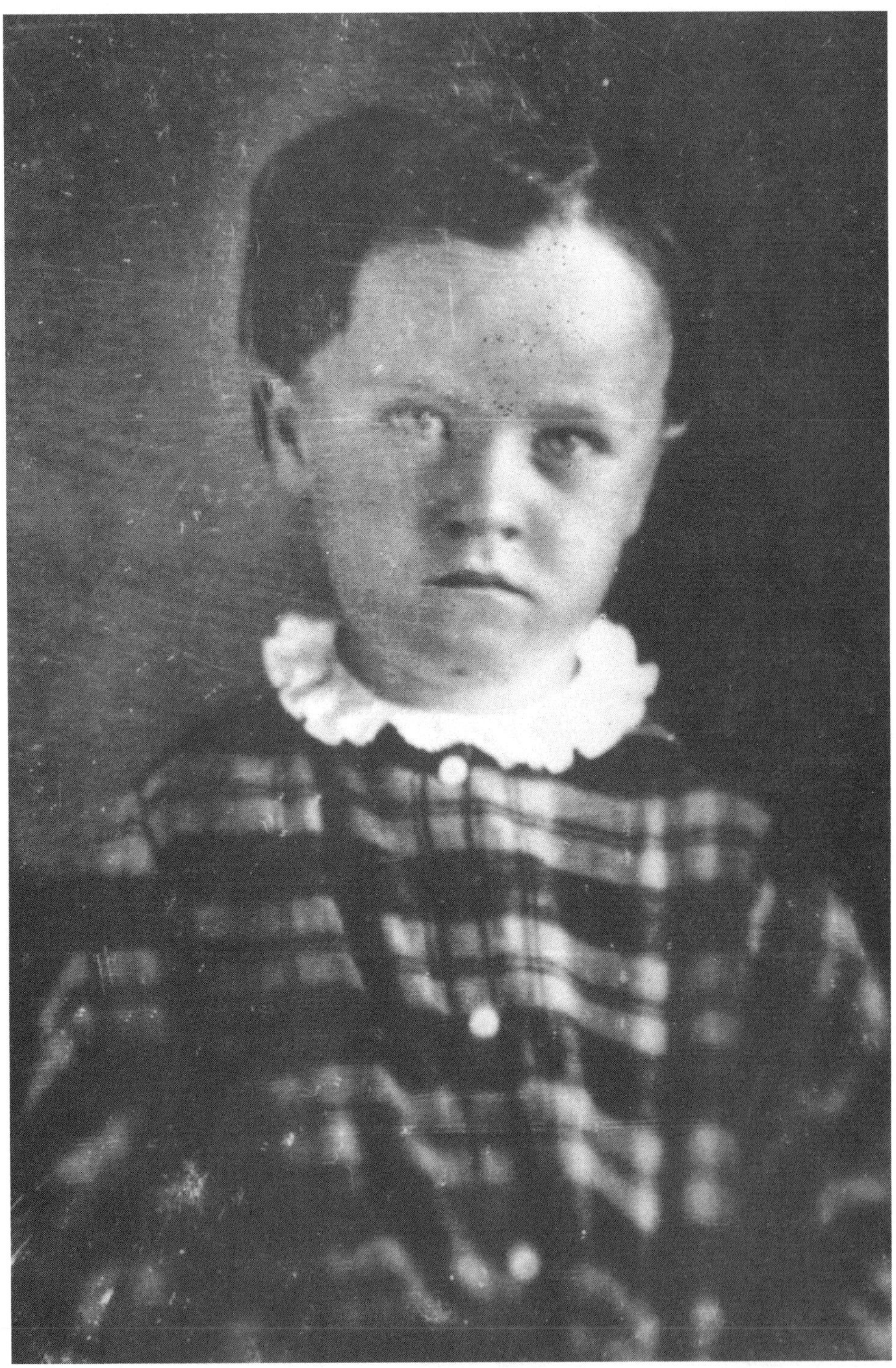

Despite being a sickly child, Alva, or Al, as Edison was known when young, had an active imagination and a curious nature that frequently landed him in trouble.

CHAPTER 2

Curiosity and Imagination

Thomas Alva Edison was born in Milan, Ohio, on February 11, 1847. He was named Thomas after one of his uncles; his middle name came from that of a close family friend. Growing up, he was never called Tom—it was always Alva or Al.

The Edison family had a colorful history. Two of Alva's forebears, his father and his great-grandfather, had each found himself on the losing side of a political conflict and had become an exile as a result of his political convictions.

In fact, at the time Alva was born, his father had been in the United States for only 10 years. In 1837, Samuel Edison was forced to flee from Canada because of his participation in a failed revolt against the British-controlled government. Running from the royal militia, he narrowly avoided arrest by crossing the border into Michigan. Within a few months, he made his way into northern Ohio and settled in the canal town of Milan, about 10 miles from the southern shore of Lake Erie.

Ironically, Sam's Dutch-born grandfather, John Edison (who spelled the name "Edeson"), had first moved the family to Canada several decades earlier because of his pro-

British sympathies. A well-to-do landowner in colonial New Jersey, he had remained loyal to the king when the American Revolution erupted in 1775. After aiding the British as a scout, he was captured by the revolutionaries and imprisoned. He would have been hanged were it not for the appeals of his wife, who had relatives in the Continental army. After the war, John's property was confiscated, and the family relocated north of the border.

More than 60 years after John Edison had moved to Canada, Sam Edison was himself an exile in the country his grandfather had been forced to leave. Fortunately, he was a skilled carpenter with an entrepreneurial bent, and he soon established himself in Milan as a lumber dealer and shingle maker. In 1839, he arranged to have his wife Nancy, whom he had married 11 years before, brought from Canada with their four children, Marion, William Pitt, Harriet, and Carlisle. He built them a cozy, red-brick house of seven rooms on a hillside overlooking the Milan canal basin.

The three-mile canal linked Milan to the Huron River, which joined Lake Erie. This little waterway, which was being dug when Sam arrived in town, was part of a national canal-building boom that had flourished in the country since the successful opening of New York's Erie Canal in 1825. By aiding transportation into the remote inner reaches of the young country, canals did much to boost settlement and trade. The canal in Milan, while much shorter than most, made the community thrive. At its height, the Ohio village was said to rank second only to Odessa, Russia, as a grain port. Hundreds of wheat-bearing wagons arrived each day to load the big ships and barges bound for the Great Lakes. And as Milan prospered, so did Sam Edison's enterprises.

Tragedy at home, however, tempered Sam's success as a Milan businessman. In 1841, six-year-old Carlisle died. Two other children—Samuel, born in 1840, and Eliza, born in 1844—each died by the time they were three years old.

Thus there was probably as much apprehension as joy in the Edison household when Thomas Alva, the seventh and last-born child, arrived early on a snowy morning in 1847. The newborn infant had an unusually large head, which caused the village doctor to fear an infection of "brain fever" (meningitis). Luckily, the physician's concern was unfounded, although respiratory ailments and earaches would torment Alva throughout his childhood.

Despite his frequent illnesses, Alva became an active child bursting with curiosity. Nancy Edison, who was well educated and devoutly religious, worried endlessly, not only about his delicate health but about his knack for getting into trouble. Spanking him with a switch she regularly retrieved from behind the family clock, she tried to keep the boy in line.

She rarely succeeded, and Alva's escapades became notorious around town. On one occasion, he nearly drowned in the canal; on another, he barely escaped suffocation after falling into a grain elevator. At the age of six, he set a fire in his father's barn "just to see what it would do," as he explained his misdeed. The flames quickly consumed the wooden structure as young Alva scrambled for safety. Sam Edison, usually an easygoing sort, marched his son to the town square and whipped him soundly in front of a large crowd.

Alva's knack for getting into trouble provided a constant source of worry for his mother Nancy, a well educated and devoutly religious woman.

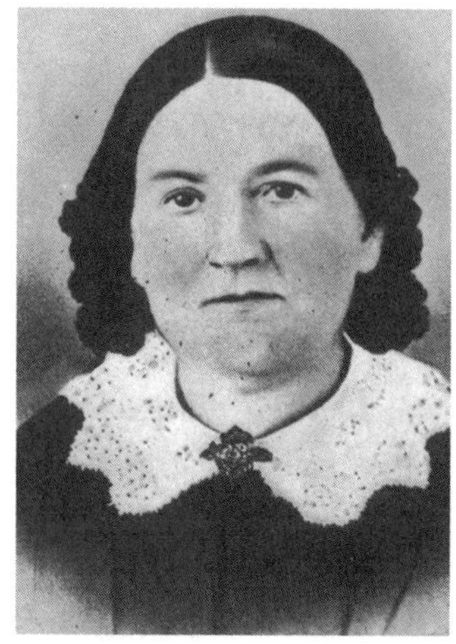

One incident, which happened at about the same time as the barn burning, had tragic consequences. As Edison later remembered, he and a playmate had gone swimming in a creek near the edge of town. The other boy was not a good swimmer and "disappeared in the creek." Alva did not know what to do. "I waited around for him to come up," he recalled, "but as it was getting dark I concluded to wait no longer and went home." Later awakened and questioned about his friend's disappearance, Alva told the adults what had happened.

A search of the creek turned up the boy's drowned body.

The scoldings and whippings that followed such episodes did not diminish Alva's curiosity. Full of questions, he was always ready to test whatever anyone told him. When he asked his mother why the goose sat on its eggs, her answer—"To hatch them"—sent him off to a neighbor's barn, where he curled up with some goose and hen eggs and tried to hatch them himself.

Alva had not yet entered school when Sam and Nancy decided to leave Milan. By 1854, the town was falling on hard times. The main reason for the decline was the railroad—a faster, more efficient form of transportation that was rapidly making canals obsolete. During the previous year, the rails had bypassed Milan in favor of a neighboring village. Soon many residents, including the Edisons, were looking elsewhere for new opportunities.

In 1837, after taking part in an unsuccessful attempt to overthrow the Canadian government, Samuel Edison was forced to flee the country and settle in the United States. He was joined by his wife and children two years later.

The state of Michigan, where Sam Edison had first entered the country, seemed like a good place to make a fresh start. Boasting rich forests and mineral deposits, the region bustled with new settlers. One of Sam's brothers was already living near the town of Port Huron, and it was there that the Edisons decided to resettle in the spring of 1854. Alva was then seven years old.

Located at the juncture of Lake Huron and the Saint Clair River, Port Huron was home to an army post named Fort Gratiot. Near the parade ground of that post was a big, ten-room house, much more spacious than the one in Milan, which became the Edison's new residence. With large windows and second-floor balconies, the house had scenic views of both the lake and the river, where commercial vessels were constantly coming and going.

The stories of Edison's life differ about the details of what Sam did for a living in Port Huron. Some accounts say that Sam ran a grocery store and dealt in lumber and real estate, while others say he worked as a carpenter and lighthouse-keeper for the army post. In any case, it seems clear that Sam liked to dabble in a variety of things but that none of them proved very profitable. As a result, the family's financial state would become shaky in the years to come.

Alva attended school for the first time in Port Huron, starting when he was about eight. His parents first enrolled him in a private school run by the Reverend George B. Engle, and later he attended the Port Huron public school. The kind of education these schools offered, in which students were expected to learn their lessons by memorizing them, had little appeal for an inquisitive dreamer like Alva Edison. His teachers failed to understand him, and his talent for mischief just made matters worse. In a typical prank, he and a public-school classmate dropped a hook and line from one of the school's second-floor windows, snagged a chicken, and proceeded to haul up the unfortunate bird. A thrashing from the principal followed—and it was only one of many.

In all, Alva probably attended school for no more than a few months. As he recalled years later, he one day overheard a teacher declare that he was "addled." Upset, he ran home and told his mother, who indignantly withdrew him from the school and vowed to teach him on her own. Although Nancy Edison was probably as strict a disciplinarian as any of Alva's other teachers, she gave him lessons that were far more stimulating. She read to him from Dickens's novels and Shakespeare's plays, from Edward Gibbon's *Decline and Fall of the Roman Empire* and David Hume's *History of England.* She also encouraged him to read on his own. He became entranced with one work in particular: *A School Compendium of Natural and Experimental Philosophy,* an elementary science text by Richard Green Parker. The book described simple experiments that Alva could perform himself, and before long he was trying them all.

Science and reading appealed to the young Edison much more than the household chores he was expected to perform, such as tending his father's vegetable garden and selling its produce. His allowance went for chemicals he purchased from a local druggist. At first he performed his experiments in his bedroom, but his chemicals made such a mess that his parents insisted he move them to the cellar. There he labeled all his bottles "poison" to keep them out of others' hands.

By the time he was 12, Alva felt the need to strike out in a new direction. Over his mother's objections, he insisted on going to work. Whatever resistance Nancy may have offered, however, was offset by a sad necessity: the Edisons could use the money. No longer the prosperous businessman he had been in Milan, Sam was now constantly in debt. So, in 1859, Alva became the family's most reliable breadwinner.

The railroad provided the future inventor with his first employment. The Grand Trunk company had just opened a line into Port Huron from Detroit, 63 miles to the south. Sam arranged for Alva to work as a candy butcher, a vendor who sold snacks and newspapers to the passengers. In later years, Edison would remember his job on the Grand Trunk Railroad as "the happiest time of my life."

Rising at six every morning, Alva drove a horse and cart to the station and boarded the train in time for its 7:15 departure. As the train puffed toward Detroit, stopping at several towns along the way, Alva walked through the three passenger coaches carrying a basket filled with his wares. "Newspapers! Apples! Sandwiches!" he shouted to the passengers huddled on wooden benches. "Molasses! Peanuts!"

Four hours after leaving Port Huron, the train arrived in Detroit. The returning train did not depart until the late afternoon, when Alva repeated his routine. It was usually 11 o'clock before the boy was in bed.

Alva's long daily layovers in Detroit expanded his sense of the world. With nearly 50,000 people, Detroit was a major shipping and industrial center buzzing with activity.

At the age of 12, after spending only a few months in school, Edison decided to take a job selling snacks and newspapers on the Grand Trunk Railroad.

Alva enjoyed visiting the city's machine shops and watching the trains being switched in the rail yard. One of his favorite haunts was the train station's telegraph office, where he gazed in fascination as the operators signaled train movements to other stations.

Detroit also nurtured his love of chemistry. One of its main industries was the production of chemicals and pharmaceuticals, so Alva had no trouble restocking the collection of bottles he kept at home. After a while, he decided to move his laboratory onto the train. With the permission of the conductor, Alexander Stevenson, he set up his chemicals in an unused corner of the baggage car and devoted his free hours to experiments.

Unfortunately, his mobile lab came to an abrupt end when some phosphorus sticks, accidentally exposed to the air, ignited and started a fire on the baggage-car floor. Helping to smother the blaze, Stevenson burned his fingers badly. At that point, he banned Alva's little laboratory from the train.

The incident became the source of a popular Edison legend. According to this story, Stevenson boxed Alva's ears to punish him for the accident, thus causing the partial deafness that plagued him throughout his life. Edison himself discounted this version, claiming that his deafness had started earlier with another incident on the train. One day, while some newspaper customers delayed him on the platform, the train began to leave the station. Dashing after it, he was spotted by Stevenson, who grabbed him by the ears and pulled him aboard. At that moment, Edison recalled, "I felt something in my ears crack and right after that I began to get deaf."

In all likelihood, however, the real culprit for Edison's deafness was not a rough encounter with a train conductor. His long history of ear infections and a possible bout of scarlet fever were probably the true causes of his hearing loss. In any case, the deafness does appear to have set in around the time he began working on the Grand Trunk Railroad. "I have not heard a bird sing since I was twelve years old," he lamented in his diary years later.

These hearing problems pushed Alva deeper into the world of books. Victor Hugo's novel *Les Misérables* became one of his favorite works. This sprawling tale, which tells of an ex-convict named Jean Valjean and his struggles against a pitiless society, no doubt appealed to a romantic streak in the young Edison. Thomas Paine's *The Age of Reason* had an even more pronounced effect on him. Recommended to him by his free-thinking father, Paine's book advanced some radical notions that fascinated Alva. Although Paine asserted the existence of God, he criticized traditional religious beliefs and teachings. Paine argued that churches were merely "human inventions set up to terrify and enslave mankind" and declared, "The world is my country; to do good my religion."

Paine's words made sense to young Edison and bolstered his growing skepticism about organized religion. His devout mother was unhappy when he stopped accompanying her to church, but there was little she could do to counter the boy's increasingly independent ways.

At 15, Alva joined the Young Men's Society of Detroit and used its library and reading room. Although he later boasted that he had read the entire library, he was stretching the truth. As he admitted to a friend in 1905, "reading the library" may have been his goal, but he gave it up after plowing through "about ten books that were pretty dry reading."

Among the volumes he claimed to have struggled with—and disliked—was Sir Isaac Newton's great theoretical opus *Philosophiae Naturalis Principia Mathematica* (Mathematical Principles of Natural Philosophy), the work that lay the foundations for modern science. Unfortunately, the only thing Edison took from it was "a distaste for mathematics from which I have never recovered."

More to his liking was Andrew Ure's *Arts, Manufactures, and Mines,* which disdained scientific theory in favor of practical knowledge. Ure ridiculed the "speculative scientists" and praised artisans and mechanics as the real bringers of progress. Ure's arguments were not lost on the young Edison, whose practical bent—the desire to make something useful—would be the hallmark of his later inventions.

While Alva's spare-time habits of reading and performing experiments sharpened his mind, his job on the train sharpened his business savvy. He proved such a successful salesman of newspapers, candies, and fruits that he expanded his business with the help of friends and of produce from his father's vegetable garden. "After being on the train for several months," Edison remembered, "I started two stores in Port Huron—one for periodicals, and the other for vegetables, butter, and berries in the season. They were attended by two boys who shared in the profits."

His entrepreneurial spirit showed itself in other ways. After the fire that sealed the fate of his mobile laboratory, he put the space in the baggage car to a different use. After acquiring a little printing press and some old type, he began to publish the weekly *Grand Trunk Herald,* which reported on small events along the Detroit–Port Huron line and sold for three cents a copy. Setting the type by hand exhausted him, however, and publication of the *Herald* ceased after only a few issues.

Still, Alva was not ready to quit publishing altogether. He turned for help to an acquaintance named Will Wright, who worked at the *Port Huron Commercial.* Alva had an idea for a new publication, and he persuaded Wright to print it. This arrangement freed Alva to concentrate on writing and editing the new paper, which he called *Paul Pry.* Filled with gossip and society news, *Paul Pry* contained one story that so enraged a Port Huron doctor that he threatened to toss Alva into the Saint Clair River. Thus, the young Edison decided that journalism was not such an attractive career after all.

Although his own publishing ventures were short-lived, Alva continued to prosper by hawking other people's newspapers. In the spring of 1862, he enjoyed his biggest success as a teenaged businessman. The Civil War had begun the previous year, and now, as its pace picked up, people everywhere sought news about it. On April 6, when Alva arrived at the offices of the *Detroit Free Press* to pick up his papers, he encountered

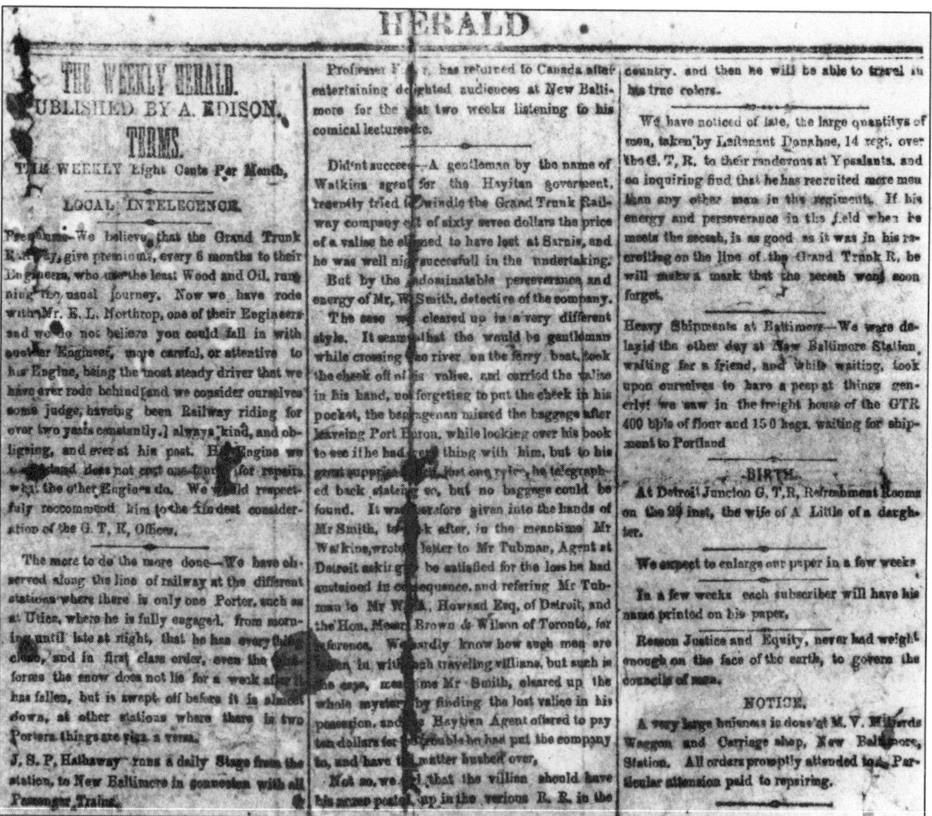

HERALD.

THE WEEKLY HERALD.
[illegible]UBLISHED BY A. EDISON.
TERMS.
THE WEEKLY Eight Cents Per Month,

LOCAL INTELEGENCE.

[illegible]—We believe, that the Grand Trunk [illegible], give premiums, every 6 months to their Engineers, who use the least Wood and Oil, running the usual journey. Now we have rode with Mr. E. L. Northrop, one of their Engineers and we do not believe you could fall in with another Engineer, more careful, or attentive to his Engine, being the most steady driver that we have ever rode behind [and we consider ourselves some judge, haveing been Railway riding for over two years constantly.] always kind, and obliging, and ever at his post. His Engine we [illegible] does not cost one-fourth for repairs what the other Engines do. We would respectfuly recommend him to the kindest consideration of the G. T. R. Officers.

The more to do the more done—We have observed along the line of railway at the different stations where there is only one Porter, such as at Utica, where he is fully engaged, from morning until late at night, that he has everything clean, and in first class order, even the [illegible] forms the snow does not lie for a week after it has fallen, but is swept off before it is almost down, at other stations where there is two Porters things are vica a versa.

J. S. P, Hathaway runs a daily Stage from the station, to New Baltimore in connection with all Passenger Trains.

Professor F[illegible]r, has returned to Canada after entertaining delighted audiences at New Baltimore for the past two weeks listening to his comical lectures[illegible].

Did'nt succeed—A gentleman by the name of Watkins agent for the Hayitan goverment, recently tried to swindle the Grand Trunk Railway company out of sixty seven dollars the price of a valise he claimed to have lost at Sarnia, and he was well nigh successfull in the undertaking. But by the indominatable perseverance and energy of Mr, W. Smith, detective of the company. The case was cleared up in a very different style. It seams that the would be gentleman while crossing the river on the ferry boat, took the check off of his valise, and carried the valise in his hand, not forgeting to put the check in his pocket, the baggageman missed the baggage after leaveing Port Huron, while looking over his book to see if he had [illegible] thing with him, but to his great surprise [illegible] just one [illegible], he telegraphed back stateing so, but no baggage could be found. It was therefore given into the hands of Mr Smith, to look after, in the meantime Mr Watkins, wrote a letter to Mr Tubman, Agent at Detroit asking to be satisfied for the loss he had sustained in consequence, and refering Mr Tubman to Mr W[illegible], Howard Esq, of Detroit, and the Hon. Messrs Brown & Wilson of Toronto, for reference. We hardly know how such men are taken in with such traveling villians, but such is the case, meantime Mr Smith, cleared up the whole mystery by finding the lost valise in his possession, and the Haytien Agent offered to pay ten dollars for the trouble he had put the company to, and have the matter hushed over.

Not so, we [illegible], that the villian should have his name posted up in the various R. R. in the country, and then he will be able to travel in his true colors.

We have noticed of late, the large quantitys of men, taken by Leitenant Donahoe, 14 regt. over the G. T. R. to their randevous at Ypsalanta, and on inquiring find that he has recruited more men than any other man in the regiment. If his energy and perseverance in the field when he meets the secesh, is as good as it was in his recruiting on the line of the Grand Trunk R, he will make a mark that the secesh wont soon forget.

Heavy Shipments at Baltimore—We were delayed the other day at New Baltimore Station, waiting for a friend, and while waiting, took upon ourselves to have a peep at things generly: we saw in the freight house of the GTR 400 bbls of flour and 150 hogs, waiting for shipment to Portland

BIRTH.

At Detroit Juncion G. T. R, Refreshment Rooms on the 29 inst, the wife of A Little of a daughter.

We expect to enlarge our paper in a few weeks

In a few weeks each subscriber will have his name printed on his paper.

Reason Justice and Equity, never had weight enough on the face of the earth, to govern the councils of men.

NOTICE.

A very large buisness is done at M. V. Millards Waggon and Carriage shop, New Baltimore, Station. All orders promptly attended to. Particular attension paid to repairing.

In 1862, at the age of 15, Edison began publishing the Grand Trunk Herald, *a weekly newspaper devoted to local news and gossip. He sold it for three cents a copy.*

a large and anxious crowd seeking word about a major engagement then underway in Tennessee. It was the battle of Shiloh, and the early reports spoke of tens of thousands of casualties.

An idea hit him. Knowing that the battle would be big news that day, he ran back to the train station and struck a deal with the telegraph operator. In exchange for a promise of free papers and magazines, the telegrapher agreed to wire a bulletin about Shiloh to all the stops along the line to Port Huron. According to the instructions Alva set forth, each stationmaster, in turn, was to then write the reports on the blackboards ordinarily used to announce train schedules.

Returning to the *Free Press* offices, he convinced the editor, Wilbur F. Storey, to let him have a thousand papers on credit. That evening, as the train rolled into each station, Alva found a huge crowd waiting to buy his papers. At the first stop, Alva was able to sell the papers for five cents each. By the time the train reached Port Huron, they were going for a quarter. Alva managed to sell every copy.

Not only had his idea worked, it had impressed him more than ever with the power of the telegraph. This marvelous device, developed in the late 1830s by Samuel F. B. Morse, had revolutionized the communications of the era. Through the mysterious force of electrical current, messages could be sent instantaneously over a distance of up to 200 miles. The technology intrigued Alva no end, and he began to think seriously about becoming a telegrapher.

Even before taking the job on the Grand Trunk Railroad, Alva had tinkered a bit with some wet-cell batteries and a crude telegraph set he had built himself. Daily exposure to the telegraph operators who worked along the train line had intensified his interest. But he needed someone to teach him the craft.

The Mount Clemens train station, where Edison took telegraphy lessons, was one of several stops along the railroad line connecting Port Huron and Detroit.

CHAPTER 3

The Tinkering Telegrapher

Alva soon found a telegraphy instructor. He was James U. MacKenzie, the stationmaster at Mount Clemens, one of the stops between Port Huron and Detroit. MacKenzie liked the young Edison, especially after a day in 1862 when Alva had snatched MacKenzie's three-year-old son off the train tracks and out of the path of a stray boxcar. Early in 1863, when Alva was 16, MacKenzie agreed to give him telegraphy lessons.

Alva was entering a fast-growing field. In the mid-19th century, the expansion of the telegraph went hand in hand with that of the railroad. With operators following the train movements and relaying them to other stations, telegraphy made rail travel safer and more efficient. As the iron network of railroads spread across the country so did the telegraph wires, strung on poles alongside the tracks.

The telegraph was revolutionizing other areas of daily life as well. Newspapers used it to relay fast-breaking stories over long distances, and it was also becoming a standard tool in the financial centers back east, where quick information meant the difference between making money or losing it. During the Civil War, the telegraph became an

invaluable aid to military operations on both sides.

In fact, at the time when Edison began to learn telegraphy, skilled operators were being recruited into the military by the hundreds. Since this left many civilian openings, Alva knew he would have no trouble finding a job. But first he had to learn from MacKenzie the intricacies of the telegraph and Morse code.

To send telegraph messages, an operator tapped on a small lever, or key, connected to an electrical circuit. Depressing the key completed the circuit; releasing the key broke it. In this way, short bursts of electricity, supplied by batteries, were transmitted along the telegraph wire to a receiver at another station. With each tap on the transmitting key, the current flowed into the receiver's electromagnet—a length of wire coiled around an iron bar—and created a small magnetic field. The magnetism in turn activated a sounding device that produced an audible click. Thus, one telegraph operator could relay a series of clicking sounds to another.

These signals would have been meaningless without Samuel Morse's ingenious code, which was based on combinations of dots and dashes. (In telegraphy, a short interval between clicks indicates a dot, a long interval a dash.) Each letter in the alphabet is assigned its own unique dot-and-dash combination. The letter *A* consists of a dot followed by a dash; the letter *B* is a dash followed by three dots; the letter *C* is a dash-dot-dash-dot combination; and so on. With Morse code, the clicks made sense, and communication became possible.

Telegraph operators in Edison's day had to be adept at sending and receiving messages with speed and accuracy. A top telegrapher could manage 40 to 50 words a minute. Receiving messages, in particular, required a good ear—the operator had to be able to distinguish the clicks and then write down the words with a pencil. It might seem that the

text continues on page 30

ELECTRICITY: A FEW KEY FACTS

Most of the inventions Thomas Edison produced during his lifetime depended in one way or another on electricity. When Edison began his career, however, this form of energy was still a mystery in many ways. Although scientists such as Michael Faraday had discovered numerous things about electricity before Edison was even born, its underlying nature remained largely unknown until the late 1890s, when experimenters began to explore the possibility that atoms—long thought to be the smallest units of matter and therefore indivisible—might be made up of even smaller particles.

Scientists gradually developed the theory that an atom consists of negatively charged particles called electrons orbiting a nucleus containing two other types of subatomic particles: protons, which have a positive charge, and neutrons, which have no charge. Electrons are now understood to be the fundamental units of electricity.

An electric current consists of a stream of freed electrons flowing through a material called a conductor. Metals such as copper and aluminum are good conductors of electricity and so are used in electrical wiring. Substances that are poor carriers of electricity—such as rubber and glass—are called insulators and so are used to protect electrical wiring.

There are various ways of creating electric current. The two sources of electricity with which Edison was most familiar were batteries and generators. Batteries convert chemical energy into electrical energy and are still used today in hundreds of devices ranging from watches to flashlights to automobiles. Whatever its type, every battery contains some combination of chemicals that react with each other in such a way that electrons are freed, and a current is produced as a result.

Generators, on the other hand, convert mechanical energy into electrical energy. The basic principle behind generators was established

ELECTRICITY: A FEW KEY FACTS

text continued from page 27

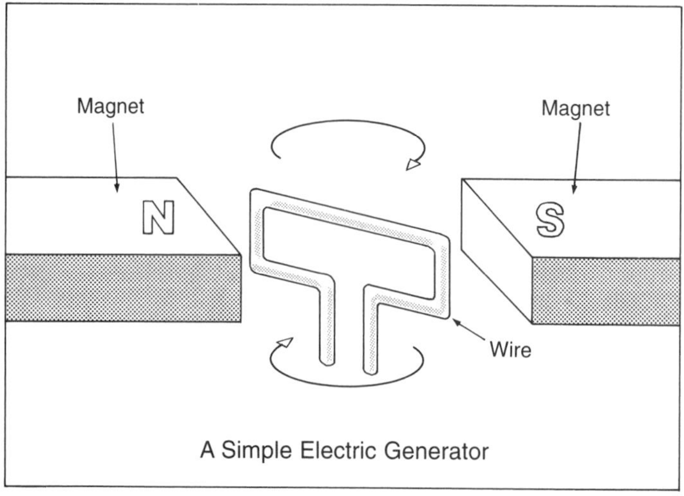

This simple diagram shows how an electric generator works. When a conductor (in this drawing, the wire loop) is rotated within a magnetic field, an electric current starts to flow through the conductor. The current, in turn, can be channelled into a circuit to which various electrical devices may be connected. The principle underlying the way generators work was discovered by Michael Faraday and is called electromagnetic induction (see page 37 for additional discussion).

in the 1830s by Faraday. He found that by the mechanical action of rotating a conductor (such as a copper wheel or loop of wire) between the poles of a magnet, an electric current is produced (or, as scientists say, induced) in the conductor. Today, more than 150 years after Faraday's experiments, this same principle is used in the giant power plants that supply electricity to millions of consumers. (Chapters 6 and 7 contain additional discussion of generators, especially the type known as dynamos, and the uses that Edison made of them.)

Generators are able to work because of a close relationship between electricity and magnetism—that phenomenon in which certain substances either attract or repel each other. Not only can magnetic fields be used to produce electric currents, but electric currents can be used to produce magnetic fields. In fact, every time electricity flows through a wire, a magnetic field is produced around the wire. A simple electromagnet can be created by coiling a length of wire around a piece of iron and attaching the ends of the wire to a source of electricity. Unlike permanent magnets (such as the naturally occurring mineral called lodestone), electromagnets work only when a current is turned on.

Whether produced by a battery or a generator, an electric current requires a complete circuit in order to flow. This means that the conducting wire must circle back to the source of electricity. Along such a circuit, various electrical devices—such as lamps and appliances—can be attached. When we switch on a lamp or other electrical device, we are completing a circuit.

Like other physical phenomena, electricity behaves in predictable ways, and so scientists have developed units of measurement and complex mathematical formulas in order to describe and manipulate it. The energy that moves electricity through a conductor is measured in volts and called electromotive force or voltage. The strength of a current, which depends on the number of electrons it contains, is expressed in amperes. The basic unit of electric power (which takes both voltage and amperage into account) is called the watt. Still another common unit of electrical measurement is the ohm, which is used to describe the resistance in a circuit. Resistance refers to those properties of a substance that restrict the flow of electricity through it, and it played an especially important role in the creation of Edison's electric light (see Chapter 6).

text continued from page 26

young Edison's hearing problems would have hindered his work as a telegrapher. In fact, he claimed, his partial deafness helped him. He could hear the clicks but not the distracting background noises.

Alva trained under MacKenzie for five months. He kept his candy butcher's job but now traveled only as far as Mount Clemens, where he got off the train for his daily lessons. MacKenzie was already teaching telegraphy to another boy, and the two youths practiced by sending messages back and forth to each other. Alva also made his own telegraph set so that he could practice back in Port Huron. Stringing a mile-long wire to the home of his friend Jim Clancy, he taught Jim the lessons MacKenzie was teaching him.

In the summer of 1863, after completing his training with MacKenzie, Alva began his telegraphy career with a part-time job at Port Huron. A corner of Thomas Walker's jewelry store doubled as the town telegraph office, and when Alva was not sending and receiving telegrams, he used space in Walker's shop to read Walker's back issues of *Scientific American* and to continue his scientific tinkering. One day a loud explosion rocked the jewelry store. A chemistry experiment had gone awry, and Alva was fired from his first job as a telegrapher almost before he had started it.

There would, however, be many other telegraph assignments over the next four years. From 1863 to 1867, the young Edison wandered from job to job as a "tramp telegrapher." His gypsy-like travels would take him to

For five months James MacKenzie, the station-master at Mount Clemens, Michigan, taught Edison the basics of telegraphy.

such places as Stratford, Ontario, in Canada; Adrian, Michigan; Toledo, Ohio; Indianapolis, Indiana; Cincinnati, Ohio; Memphis, Tennessee; Louisville, Kentucky; and New Orleans, Louisiana.

It was an adventurous life, if not a glamorous one. Telegraphers worked long hours in filthy, cramped, cluttered offices. They slept in seedy boardinghouses. Drinking whiskey, chewing tobacco, and swapping bawdy stories were among their favorite pastimes. Alva no doubt acquired many such vices, although his system could not abide liquor: one drink would put him to sleep.

During his telegraphy days, Alva formed several lasting friendships, but by and large he was not popular with the other operators. For one thing, he loved to play practical jokes, and his co-workers were his favorite victims. Once in Cincinnati, he wired a Ruhmkorff induction coil (a device for boosting the voltage from a battery) to a water trough used by the railroad employees. Alva thought it was great fun to watch an unsuspecting man receive an electric jolt when he reached into the trough to wash his hands. It did not take long before Alva's pranks stopped being funny—except, of course, to Alva.

His relations with his supervisors were no better. He was often fired, either for inattention to his job or for causing some mishap. In Stratford, Ontario, he was blamed for a minor train accident; facing punishment, he lit out for the American border at the first opportunity, much as his father had done a quarter century earlier. A couple of years later, while experimenting in the Louisville telegraph office, he dropped a container of battery acid, which ate through the floor and ruined the furniture and carpet in the office below. His boss sent him packing, declaring that the company "needed operators, not experimenters."

Alva took these firings in stride. Indeed, his vagabond's life was the typical lot of telegraph operators, who might take off at the slightest whim for parts unknown. At one point, Alva seriously considered going to Brazil in search of fresh opportunities. Luckily he changed his mind: The two acquaintances who did attempt the journey died of yellow fever in a Mexican port.

For a mind as restless and imaginative as Edison's, much of what telegraphers did was pure tedium. Thus he often applied his ingenuity to finding ways to make his job easier. While working at the Stratford station, for example, he was assigned to a late shift during which only two trains passed through. The job was so uneventful and monotonous that one of his primary responsibilities was sending a telegraph signal to the main office every hour—just to show that he was at his post and not asleep. To allow himself to take naps, he devised a clockwork mechanism and rigged it to the telegraph key. Every hour it sent the signal for him.

The life of a telegraph operator offered Edison a chance to travel and see a large part of the United States. The work also left him with plenty of free time to experiment and study.

Edison created an even more ingenious device in Indianapolis. He was still a novice operator and not very

good at taking messages. Amid the office clutter he found an old-fashioned Morse register that no one was using. This device was a relic of earlier days, before operators became adept at receiving messages by ear. The register actually recorded the incoming dots and dashes by using a needle to emboss them on a strip of paper. Alva found a way to run the strip through a second machine whose speed he could regulate. Thus, if a message came in at a speed faster than he could handle, he could record it and play it back at a slower speed.

The device did wonders for the legibility and accuracy of his copy. His transcriptions were so "clean and beautiful," he remembered, that they were hung up for all to admire. The boss marveled at Alva's work, unaware of how Alva had managed the trick. Unfortunately, during a Presidential election one night, the copy came "pouring in at top speed, until we found ourselves two hours behind." His gadget discovered, Edison was forbidden further use of his "automatic repeater," which was blamed for slowing down his work.

In Memphis, he tried to reintroduce the device for a different purpose. In those days, telegraphic communication was hindered by the fact that the signals could travel only so far. To send a message farther than 200 miles, an operator at an intermediate station had to write it down and retransmit it down the line. This method was slow and allowed a lot of human error to creep in—several operators handling one message inevitably made mistakes. Alva tried to solve the problem with his repeater. After recording the message on the incoming line, he fed the paper strip into a transmitter on a different line. The message could thus be passed along mechanically with no loss of accuracy.

Instead of being praised for his ingenuity, Alva was fired. According to one version of the story, the Memphis supervisor had been working on the same problem when young Edison came along and solved it. Angry at being bested by a subordinate, he showed Alva the door.

Another account suggests that Edison made his Memphis boss angry by spending too much of his time trying to invent a duplex, an improved telegraph that would allow two messages to be transmitted simultaneously over the same wire in different directions. If he could create such a device, Edison realized, it would be a real breakthrough, doubling the volume of messages that a telegraph company could handle. His boss thought the scheme was harebrained, however. "Any damn fool ought to know that a wire can't be worked both ways at the same time," he told Alva.

Edison would hear this sort of thing countless times in the years to come. Tackling some difficult invention, he would encounter a chorus of naysayers who believed that he was attempting the impossible. Fortunately, since he trusted no one's instincts better than his own, he did not listen to them.

Despite his frequent run-ins with supervisors, Edison eventually earned a first-class rating as a telegrapher. The pay was not bad for that era—$125 a month. But Edison spent most of his income on equipment for his experiments and borrowed money whenever he ran short—which was often. Increasingly, he discovered, his heart was not in telegraphy. He wanted to be an inventor.

His appetite for invention was further whetted by a brief visit to Boston, Massachusetts, near the end of 1866. With another telegrapher, Sam Ropes, he had been working for some time on a device that would print telegraphic messages in regular letters on a strip of paper. Ropes eventually left for Boston, where he attracted the interest of two businessmen. Edison followed him to Boston and on January 1, 1867, signed a contract to produce the telegraphic printer. His pay, upon completion of the device, was to be $250.

It is not clear whether Edison ever received the money. Nevertheless, the episode revealed that some people were willing to compensate him for his inventions. Perhaps he could even make a living at it.

In the fall of 1867, Edison returned to Port Huron, where he encountered an unhappy household. Grief and worry had taken its toll on his mother. By now Nancy had lost four children—Alva's sister Harriet had died just four years earlier. Meanwhile, his brother Pitt, 37 years old and still living in Port Huron, demonstrated little aptitude for work or business. Nancy feared that Alva would follow a similar path. Never a cheerful woman, Nancy was now showing signs of mental illness. Sam was unable to deal with his wife's deteriorating condition and seldom spent time at home.

In such an environment, Alva did not want to stick around for long. He sent out inquiries to various telegraphers he knew, asking about fresh job opportunities. In exchange for repairing a telegraph line, he received a train ticket from his old employer, the Grand Trunk Railroad, and set out eastward in January 1868. He arrived in Montreal in the middle of a blizzard. A telegrapher named Stanton, whom he had known in Cincinnati, found him a room at a wretched, unheated boardinghouse. He was low on cash, and it was running out fast.

Edison's luck changed when one of his job inquiries paid off. Milt Adams, another crony from his Cincinnati days, wired him from Boston with news of an opening at the local office of Western Union, the largest of the telegraph companies. Edison was already familiar with Boston from his brief visit a year earlier, and he departed for the Massachusetts capital immediately.

Arriving in Boston and presenting himself at Western Union, Edison remembered, he found that his appearance "caused much mirth." The Boston telegraphers, a well-dressed, well-spoken, and rather snooty bunch, considered Edison the epitome of a country rube. Laughing at his ill-fitting clothes, midwestern accent, and the tobacco wad in his mouth, they were determined to give him a rough initiation into their ranks.

They assigned him to a wire that received news copy from New York. As the men gathered around in eager anticipation, Edison knew that something was afoot and soon found out what it was. The sender in New York, a fellow named Hutchison, was one of the company's fastest. Dispatching the copy slowly at first, Hutchison began to pick up speed until the sounder was clicking furiously.

But Edison's receiving skills, which included several tricks and shortcuts, were well honed by this point. He had little trouble keeping up with Hutchison and even paused a time or two to sharpen his pencil. When Edison decided that the fun had gone far enough, he broke in on the wire and sent Hutchison a mocking message: "Say, young man, change off and send with your other foot."

He had passed that test, but in the weeks ahead, his playful nature and rebellious streak often strained the patience of his supervisors and fellow operators. Among the shortcuts he had devised for taking messages and keeping up with fast senders, such as Hutchison, was to write in a very small hand so that he spent little time forming each letter. This resulted in copy that required a magnifying glass to read. When his supervisor objected, he responded by taking down a message in a hand so enormous that only a few words filled a page. This stunt got him demoted.

Edison also delighted in the reactions he drew from his co-workers when he played practical jokes. One night he fixed the telegraph keys so that they stuck. On another occasion, he wired the water bucket to a battery so that anyone taking a drink received a shock. A fellow operator, enraged by Edison's pranks, flung a heavy glass insulator at his head, barely missing him.

Despite the strained relations with his boss and the other telegraphers, Edison found Boston to be one of the most stimulating places he had ever lived. Because Boston was where the Industrial Revolution had its start in America, it teemed with tinkerers of every description, making it the country's center of invention. Edison liked to visit the Court Street shop of Charles Williams, Jr., which made telegraphic equipment and other electrical devices. He bought supplies there and spent hours chatting with the young inventors who used rooms in the shop for their experiments.

He continued his own experiments and purchased a second-hand copy of Michael Faraday's three-volume work, *Experimental Researches in Electricity*. Although the Englishman Faraday, like Edison, came from a poor family and had little formal education, he had made some of the most important discoveries in electrical science. Among these were the laws of electrolysis, which deal with the chemical reactions that occur when an electric current passes through certain substances, and the principles of electromagnetic induction, which describe how a magnetic field generated by one electric current can produce a secondary current in a nearby conductor. Faraday's clear and simple explanations of his experiments captivated Edison. The tinkering telegrapher had a new hero.

The life and work of the English scientist Michael Faraday, who was born to a poor family and received little formal schooling, provided inspiration to Edison.

Reflecting on Faraday's accomplishments, Edison reportedly turned to his roommate, Milt Adams, and said, "I am now twenty-one. I may live to be fifty. Can I get as much done as he did? I have got so much to do, and life is so short. I am going to hustle."

EDISON'S

ELECTRIC PEN and PRESS

COPIES FROM A SINGLE WRITING.

THE ELECTRIC PEN AND DUPLICATING PRESS

Was invented three years ago. Many thousands are now in use in the United States, Canada, Great Britain, France, Germany, Russia, Australia, New Zealand, Cuba, Brazil, China, Japan, and other countries.

Stencils can be made with the Electric Pen nearly as fast as writing can be done with an ordinary Pen. From 1,000 to 15,000 impressions can be taken from each stencil, by means of the Duplicating Press, at the speed of five to fifteen per minute.

The apparatus is used by the United States, City and State Governments, Railroad, Steamboat and Express Companies, Insurance and other Corporations, Colleges and Schools, Churches, Sabbath Schools, Societies, Bankers, Real Estate Dealers, Lawyers, Architects, Engineers, Accountants, Printers, and Business Firms in every department of trade.

It is especially valuable for the cheap and rapid production of all matter requiring duplication, such as Circulars, Price Lists, Market Quotations, Business Cards, Autographic Circular Letters and Postal Cards, Pamphlets, Catalogues, Ruled and Blank Forms, Lawyers' Briefs, Contracts, Abstracts, Legal Documents, Freight Tariffs, Time Tables, Invoices, Labels, Letter, Bill and Envelope Heads, Maps, Tracings, Architectural and Mechanical Drawings, Plans and Specifications, Bills of Fare, Music, Insurance Policies, Cypher Books, Cable and Telegraphic Codes, Financial Exhibits, Property Lists, Manifests, Inventories, Schedules, Shipping Lists, College and School Documents, Rolls, Examination Questions, Examples, Illustrations, Scholars' Reports, Lecture Notes, Regulations, Blanks, Official Notices, Mailing Lists, Committee Reports, Sermons, Lectures, Pastoral Information, Manuscripts, Journals, Fac-Similies of Papers, Drawings, Hieroglyphics, Programmes, Designs, etc.

Circulars prepared with the Electric Pen pass through the mails as third class matter at one cent per ounce or fraction thereof. Additional information and samples of work furnished on application.

PRICES—No. 1 Outfit, with 7×11 Press, $40.00.
" 2 " " 9×11 " 50.00.
" 3 " " 9×14 " 60.00.

Sent C.O.D., or on Receipt of Price.

GEO. H. BLISS. GENERAL MANAGER, 220 TO 232 KINZIE STREET, CHICAGO.

LOCAL AGENCY, 142 La Salle Street, Chicago.
DOMINION AGENCY, 44 Church Street, Toronto, Ont.

PHILADELPHIA AGENCY, 628 Chestnut St., Philadelphia.
GEN'L EASTERN AGENCY, 20 New Church St., New York.

An advertisement for Edison's electric pen, which used a pulsating, needle-like tip to make impressions on a waxed-paper stencil. The stencil could then be used to produce multiple copies of a document.

CHAPTER

4

The Budding Inventor

Edison was, in fact, wasting little time making a start as an inventor. After only three months in Boston, he produced a duplex telegraph that worked well enough to impress two experts in the field, Franklin L. Pope and James Ashley, co-founders of the *Telegrapher,* a New York-based trade journal, which carried a lengthy article about Edison's device in April 1868.

At least two other inventors, Moses Farmer and Joseph Stearns, had already created working duplexes. But the publicity in the *Telegrapher*, as well as other trade papers, made Edison a minor celebrity in the field, and he soon set up his own workshop with several other operators, including Milt Adams. He continued to work an evening shift at Western Union and experimented during the day.

Perfecting his duplex was just one of his projects. Another project was improving the stock ticker, a telegraphic device that had recently come into use in the New York financial world. The stock ticker reported minute-to-minute changes in gold and stock-market prices to brokers and other businessmen. The device was so named because its receiver used a type wheel that made a ticking sound as it printed the price fluctuations on a moving strip of paper. Edison became interested in the stock ticker through his association with Pope, an employee of a gold-price reporting service in New York. Pope's boss, Samuel S. Laws, had pioneered the use of the telegraph in the financial world, and Pope, in turn, had made several improvements in the device. By the late 1860s, the Laws company had numerous subscribers to its service.

Inspired by their success, Edison joined with several other telegraphers in setting up a gold reporting service in Boston. They soon had a number of customers, including Kidder, Peabody & Company, a banking firm, and the D. N. Skillings Oil Company.

In January 1869, Edison quit his job at Western Union. Like many others, he had been making use of company equipment during off-hours to perform experiments. When William Orton, the new Western Union president, banned the practice, Edison decided to strike out on his own. A notice in the *Telegrapher* announced: "T. A. Edison has resigned his situation in the Western Union office, Boston, and will devote his full time to bringing out inventions." Edison already had high hopes for two inventions: his duplex and an electric vote recorder.

With Pope's help, Edison obtained permission from the Atlantic and Pacific Telegraph Company to use one of its lines to test his duplex. In May, he and Pope tried to establish communications with each other over a line connecting New York City and Rochester, New York. The duplex, which had performed well enough in Edison's workshop, failed when it was tried over long-distance lines. Disgusted, Edison returned to Boston.

The vote recorder was also a failure—not because it did not work, but because no one wanted it. Edison got the idea for the machine while working as a telegrapher. In transcribing news copy about congressional proceedings, he had noticed how much time seemed to be wasted whenever a roll-call vote was taken. The name of each senator or representative was announced one by one, and each "yea" or "nay" was recorded by hand. To Edison, this seemed like an extraordinarily inefficient process, so he built a machine, based on the telegraph, that would tally the votes automatically. With Edison's electric vote recorder, a lawmaker could simply press a button labelled yes or no on his desk, and the totals would be registered almost immediately at the front of the chamber.

In 1869, Edison received his first patent for this invention, an electric vote recorder. However, the machine failed to attract the interest of any legislative body.

For this invention, Edison received his first patent, which he applied for in November 1868 and was awarded on June 1, 1869. Unfortunately, he discovered that a successful patent application did not guarantee the success of the invention. Neither the Massachusetts legislature nor the United States Congress showed any interest in the vote recorder. As Edison learned, it was an accepted practice in such bodies to filibuster, a process in which lawmakers who oppose a particular bill use various delaying tactics to block its passage. In one of these tactics, opponents of the legislation will demand time-consuming roll-call votes on one irrelevant motion after another. Edison's machine, by speeding up the vote-taking process, would blunt the effectiveness of this political weapon—something most legislators were reluctant to do.

Edison vowed right then that he would only make inventions for which there was a ready demand. In later years, he counted his experience with the vote recorder as one of the most important lessons he ever learned.

The failure of his duplex, meanwhile, had pushed Edison deeply into debt, and he found that no one in Boston wanted to back his inventions. His little gold-price reporting service, plagued by equipment breakdowns, was not going well either. But Edison was nothing if not a persistent optimist. Borrowing the money for boat fare, he decided to try his luck in New York City. It was now the summer of 1869.

A steamship left him, penniless and hungry, at a Hudson River dock on Manhattan's West Side. Exploring the crowded streets, Edison managed to talk a tea seller into giving him a sample package of high-quality tea, which he exchanged at a restaurant for a meal of baked apple dumplings and coffee. His stomach full, he set off in search of a former acquaintance in the hope of finding a place to stay the night. The friend was not home, and Edison spent his first night in New York on the streets.

He soon called on Franklin Pope at the offices of Samuel Laws's company in the Wall Street area. Though the Laws firm had no immediate job openings, Pope allowed Edison to sleep in the battery room and loaned him a few dollars to tide him over.

During non-working hours, Edison made a thorough inspection of Laws's equipment and familiarized himself with the transmitter that sent out gold-price information to Laws's various subscribers. This knowledge would shortly come in handy.

One day the office fell into an uproar. The transmitter had stopped, and Pope was not around. All over the financial district, the brokers who subscribed to Laws's service sent messengers to the company to find out what was going on. Chaos broke out as the boys elbowed their way into the office, shouting and screaming. Laws himself was frantic, but Edison kept his head. With an outsider's calm detachment, he saw that a broken spring had jammed two gear wheels in the transmitter. He told Laws that he could fix it.

"Fix it! Fix it!" Laws shouted back at him. Within two hours, Edison had repaired the machine. There was still a problem, however. The receivers at all the brokerage houses had gone wild when the transmitter stopped and had to be reset by hand. Edison informed Laws that he could devise a unison stop mechanism that would shut down all the receivers simultaneously should a transmitter failure happen again. This would eliminate the necessity of resetting them. Impressed, Laws questioned Edison further and offered him a position.

Laws hired Edison at $225 a month, but the promise of security was fleeting. In late August, Laws decided to pursue a full-time career in law and sold his gold-reporting service to his chief competitor, the Gold & Stock Telegraph Company. Apparently, one reason Gold & Stock bought out Laws's company was to gain control of the unison stop device that Edison had just invented! Thus, Edison's ingenuity may have helped cost him his job.

Never one to brood for long over a setback, Edison soon entered into a partnership with Pope. As they announced in the *Telegrapher,* they were establishing themselves as "Electrical Engineers and a General Telegraphic Agency." Pope handled the business affairs of the little company, while Edison was its "mechanic." James Ashley, the editor of the *Telegrapher,* was a silent partner in the firm and made sure that it received a lot of publicity.

Edison worked at making and improving telegraphic devices in a shop the company rented in Jersey City, New Jersey, just across the Hudson River from New York. He roomed with Pope's parents in nearby Elizabeth, New Jersey, and joined Pope for breakfast each morning before setting to work.

Edison had, in effect, returned to his roots. New Jersey was where his great-grandfather John had established the family on the North American continent in the early 1700s. And New Jersey would be, in the years to come, the state most closely identified with the inventing career of Thomas Alva Edison.

In 1870, at the age of 23, Edison had set up a shop in Jersey City, New Jersey, where he worked at making and improving telegraphic devices.

With little money, the company struggled along for several months. Edison produced a number of promising devices, notably improved stock tickers, for which the company sought patents. Meanwhile, the company set up a gold-price information service in New York similar to the one Edison had established in Boston.

By the spring of 1870, however, the Gold & Stock Company was anxious to buy the Edison-Pope-Ashley concern. More than anything else, the bigger firm wanted the patent rights to Edison's inventions. Pope negotiated the deal with Marshall Lefferts, the head of Gold & Stock, for a total purchase price of $15,000, to be paid out in several installments. Edison's share of the first payment came to $1,500.

Edison felt shortchanged by the arrangement, since he had done most of the work. Then, when he tried to cash his check at a bank, he was sure he had been cheated. The teller handed the check back to him and said something that Edison, with his poor hearing, could not understand. Confused and distressed, he returned to the Gold & Stock offices and confronted Lefferts about the check. Lefferts looked at the check, chuckled, and told Edison that all he needed to do was endorse it.

Lefferts probably saw Edison as a bit of a country bumpkin, but he recognized the young man's brilliance as an inventor. He established Edison in a partnership with one of his relatives, a machinist named William Unger. The new firm of Edison and Unger set up shop in Newark, New Jersey, to develop stock tickers for Gold & Stock.

Within a few months, Edison had many new projects going and was unloading a few old ones. He severed what ties remained with his partners in Boston and eventually did the same with Pope and Ashley. Meanwhile, he entered into arrangements with several investors who were planning a new company. Among these men were Daniel Craig, the former head of the Associated Press; George Harrington, who had served as assistant secretary of the treasury under President Abraham Lincoln; and Josiah Reiff, an ex-army colonel who was now treasurer of the Kansas-Pacific Railroad. For their new business venture, these men and their partners needed Edison to make improvements in an automatic telegraph system that had been developed by George Little, another New Jersey-based inventor.

With the automatic system, Morse-code messages were punched into a strip of paper using a typewriter-like machine. The strip was then fed into a high-speed transmitter that could send messages at rates of 100 words per minute or more—much faster than any human operator. Little's system had many problems, however. Among other "bugs," the machine that perforated the paper strips operated too slowly, and the system could not send messages over distances of more than 200 miles. With a confidence that was fast becoming his trademark, Edison declared that he could fix these problems.

To perfect and manufacture the devices for the newly incorporated Automatic Telegraph Company, Edison began outfitting a second workshop in Newark. It was much bigger than the one he still maintained with Unger. A wealthy man, Harrington provided the money for this ambitious new operation, christened the American Telegraph Works.

Not surprisingly, Marshall Lefferts of Gold & Stock was not happy when he learned about Edison's second shop. To reassure him, Edison promised to deliver a stock ticker better than any yet invented. Lefferts and Edison agreed on a price of $30,000, to be paid in shares of company stock if the device proved a success.

Soon Edison was also running into problems with his sponsors at the Automatic Telegraph Company. Work on the automatic progressed slowly, and Edison was spending Harrington's money all too freely. Harrington threatened to close the American Telegraph Works if Edison did not show results quickly. By the end of 1870, Edison managed to produce some working models of the system that kept Harrington at bay a little longer.

In April 1871, sad news from home interrupted Edison's intense schedule: his mother had died. He returned to Port Huron for the funeral but was back in Newark within a few days, pushing himself as hard as ever.

Throughout the next few months, the battles between the inventor and the Automatic Telegraph Company officials continued. Distressed by the mounting expenses and the inefficient way Edison was running the works, Harrington hired a shop supervisor in October. Edison indignantly resigned.

Fortunately, his other enterprise, the firm of Edison and Unger, was doing well. Gold & Stock had been absorbed into Western Union that spring, and the merger meant big money for Edison. Western Union wanted 1,200 of his stock tickers, an order worth $78,000.

With so much going on, it is surprising that Edison had time for anything besides work. While it is true that he often put in 16-hour days, he did manage to squeeze in a few visits to New York, where he enjoyed the restaurants, plays, and variety shows.

Toward the end of 1871, a young woman had caught his eye—a pretty 16-year-old named Mary Stilwell. According to one account of their courtship, Edison met her through one of the employees in his workshop and helped her land a job as a transmitter operator at Gold & Stock, which was rapidly expanding its business as a Western Union subsidiary. Since Edison often visited the Gold & Stock offices during his trips to New York, he had many opportunities to admire Mary. He was shy around women, however, and unsure of how to approach her. Often he simply stood and stared at her in silence while she nervously tried to concentrate on her work. Finally, as legend has it, he grew bold enough to ask her what she thought of him.

Edison's improved stock ticker was the first of his inventions that had widespread commercial appeal. Western Union purchased 1,200 stock tickers for a total cost of $78,000.

Mary confessed that he frightened her. As she stammered, Edison broke in: "Don't be in a hurry about telling me. It doesn't matter much, unless you want to marry me." Mary quickly warmed to Edison. Since she lived in Newark, not far from his shop, they sometimes crossed the Hudson on the ferry together. Coming from a large, middle-class family, Mary discovered that her background was similar to Edison's. No doubt his growing reputation as a brilliant inventor added to his attractiveness. Before long he was taking her to music halls and buying her presents. They married on Christmas Day, 1871.

To her dismay, Mary found that the attentiveness Edison had shown during their courtship vanished once they tied the knot. He now spent most of his time at his shop, often working until the early hours of morning. One source of tension was Edison's frustration at how little his new bride understood of his work. A few weeks after their wedding, in the midst of making notes on an experiment, he suddenly scribbled an aside: "Mrs. Mary Edison my wife Dearly Beloved cannot invent worth a damn!"

Neglected and lonely, Mary fell into a pattern of extravagant spending, proving no better at managing money than her husband. In business, Edison had developed the practice of leaving bills unpaid until his creditors were practically pounding at the door. Sadly, Mary followed his example. Using charge accounts Edison established for her at various stores, she indulged her tastes for expensive clothes, candy, and other extravagances. Whenever Edison gave her money, she simply bought more things with it instead of settling outstanding bills. It was not the happiest of marriages, and the only way Edison seemed capable of responding to its problems was to bury himself more deeply in his work.

For the next two years, Edison had no trouble staying busy. Performing best when he had many things to do, he found that the pursuit of one invention fed his fertile imagination and produced countless ideas for other inventions. Still in his twenties, Edison was now the foremost expert on the technical aspects of telegraphy, and his experiments during these years embraced every branch of the field: stock tickers, automatic telegraphs, and duplexes. In 1872 and 1873, he applied for nearly 60 patents.

But inventing cost money, and it was in his business

Edison's first wife, Mary, was only 16 when they married in 1871.

relations that Edison often got into trouble. In 1872, he ended his partnership with William Unger and took on a new partner, Joseph T. Murray. He had to borrow heavily to purchase Unger's share of the Newark shop, and Murray was as bad a business manager as Edison. Limping along under a heavy burden of debt, the Edison-Murray concern more than once approached the brink of ruin.

Such financial problems led Edison to strike deals with competing interests. In general, he did not care who provided the money for his inventions so long as someone provided it. He adopted a casual attitude about contracts—an attitude that would, unfortunately, entangle him in lawsuits throughout his career.

Late in 1872, the Automatic Telegraph Company lured Edison back into its fold. The struggling firm hoped to challenge Western Union's dominance of the telegraph industry, but to do so it desperately needed Edison's technical expertise. Edison repaid Automatic's confidence by making major improvements in the company's devices. During the summer of 1873, he even sailed to England to promote its system with the British Post Office.

At the same time, however, Edison continued to work for Western Union by producing printing telegraphs for its Gold & Stock subsidiary. He also approached William Orton, the Western Union president, about his new ideas in duplex telegraphy. Western Union already had the rights to Joseph Stearns's duplex, which was much like the one Edison had developed in Boston. The Stearns duplex could send two messages in opposite directions over one wire simultaneously. Edison now told Orton that he could invent a duplex capable of transmitting two messages in the same direction.

Intrigued by the idea, Orton allowed Edison to use the Western Union shop to build and test his devices. Edison's backers at Automatic Telegraph were untroubled by this arrangement at first, believing that they would hold the rights to any of Edison's new telegraphic inventions. But they became more concerned as Edison's ideas expanded. By 1874 the inventor was hard at work on a quadruplex—a device that could handle four messages at once, two in each direction. This invention promised an enormous increase in the volume of telegrams that could be accommodated by existing wires.

So important was the quadruplex that the question of who would own it quickly became critical. Heavily in debt, Edison at first pinned his hopes on Western Union and even agreed to let one of its officials, George Prescott, be named as a co-inventor.

During the summer of 1874, Edison successfully

demonstrated his quadruplex to Western Union. He signed a contract with the company, much to the chagrin of the Automatic Telegraph officials. But Orton wanted to purchase Edison's device as cheaply as possible and haggled with him for months over the price. In doing so, Orton angered Edison and drove him into the arms of a sworn enemy of Western Union.

That enemy was Jay Gould, a shrewd if unscrupulous financier who had amassed a huge fortune through his wheelings and dealings on Wall Street. Gould wanted to dominate the telegraph and railroad industries and was planning to buy out the Automatic Telegraph Company as part of his grand scheme. He already owned the Atlantic and Pacific Telegraph Company and held a controlling interest in the Union Pacific Railroad. Acquiring Automatic's lines—and the Edison patents it owned—would greatly strengthen his hand. If he could claim the quadruplex as well, he would indeed pose a formidable threat to Western Union, which was controlled by his archrival, Cornelius Vanderbilt.

As Gould and his associates plotted the purchase of Automatic, they also approached Edison, who gave Gould a private demonstration of the quadruplex on December 20, 1874. Feeling that he had been treated unfairly by Western Union, Edison was ready to do business with the wily financial lord.

A few days later, Josiah Reiff negotiated the sale of the Automatic Telegraph Company to Gould. Reiff also assured Gould that Edison's contract with Western Union for the quadruplex was invalid.

On January 4, 1875, Edison visited Gould at his New York mansion and agreed to sell him the quadruplex for $100,000. He received more than $20,000 in cash as well as $10,000 worth of Union Pacific bonds. The rest of his payment was to be 3,000 shares of stock in the Atlantic and Pacific Telegraph Company.

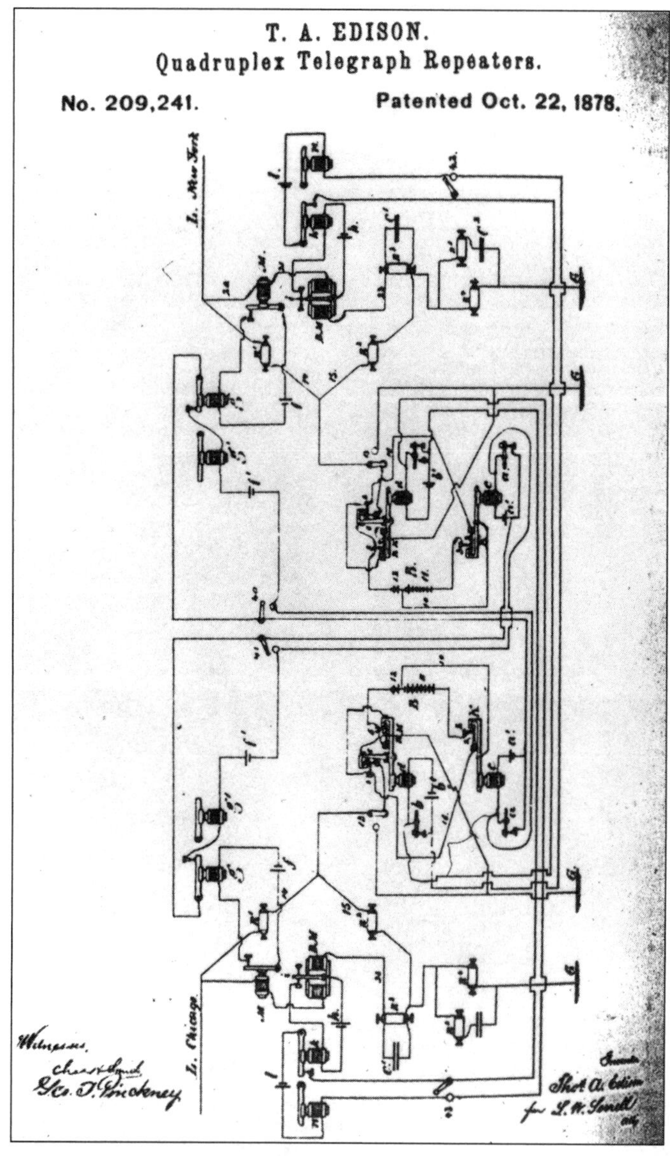

The quadruplex telegraph repeater permitted four messages to be sent over one wire at the same time. This patent drawing illustrates the complex circuitry of the device.

The deals touched off a complicated legal battle in which ownership of the quadruplex became a major bone of contention. When it appeared that Western Union would get the quadruplex, Gould used the dispute as an excuse to renege on his promises to Edison and the shareholders of Automatic Telegraph. He did pay Harrington the sum of $106,000 but withheld from the others the payments they were supposed to have received for the sale of Automatic. Reiff, Edison, and the other investors in Automatic took action against Gould in a lawsuit that would drag on for years.

Eventually, Edison received payment from Western Union for the quadruplex (a payment he had to share with Prescott). But in the end, the real winner was Jay Gould. By 1881 Gould's accumulation of power would be complete: he would take control of Western Union and reign over the telegraph industry until his death 11 years later.

Despite all the legal wrangling that erupted in 1875, Edison's inventive imagination was as active as ever. In addition to various innovations in the telegraphic field, he invented an electric perforating pen for use in copying office documents. The pen, which was powered by a tiny electric motor connected to a battery, featured a pulsating, needle-like tip. The user, handling the device like an ordinary ink pen, could then write on a sheet of waxed paper. Instead of making ink impressions, however, the electric pen produced a series of tiny perforations, thus turning the waxed paper into a stencil. Ink could then be pressed through this stencil onto sheets of paper to produce multiple copies of a document.

Compared to the quadruplex, devices such as the electric pen were minor inventions, yet they demonstrated the ever-widening range of Edison's interests. In the years ahead, Edison's remarkable ability to do many things at once would become one of his trademarks. Of the numerous concerns he had on his mind as 1875 drew to a close, the foremost was relocating his operations.

CHAPTER

5

The Wizard

As 1876 approached, Edison was anxious to leave Newark. It was an expensive place to live, and he and Mary did not even own their own home. His wife had given birth to their first child, Marion, in February 1873; now a second baby was on the way. Not only did they need living quarters bigger than the apartment they were renting, but Edison wanted a workshop away from the urban bustle—a place where he could invent without distraction.

From one of his employees Edison heard about a quiet little farming community called Menlo Park, 12 miles south of Newark. Property there was cheap, and on December 29, 1875, Edison signed the papers for the purchase of a house and pasture. They were located near a railroad line that led to Jersey City, which meant that Edison could easily travel to New York whenever the need arose.

Before long, a frame building, 100 feet long and 30 feet wide, was under construction in the Edison pasture. The Menlo Park old-timers may have thought at first that it was going to be a barn, but as the two-story, clapboard structure took shape, it assumed a closer resemblance to a meeting hall. The villagers were probably even more puzzled when

Edison's complex in Menlo Park, New Jersey. The long, narrow building served as the laboratory; the building in front served as the library and office; and the machine shop was located in the rear.

all sorts of boxes began arriving in horse-drawn wagons and were carried into the building.

It was to be the world's first industrial laboratory. Edison, having dissolved his partnership with Joseph Murray in Newark, was transferring all his operations and equipment to Menlo Park. With little more than a dozen men, he planned to turn out inventions by the score from this plain, unpretentious structure. The first floor contained a library, drafting room, and office. The second floor was a long, open room crammed with shelves and tables bearing chemicals, machines, batteries, and electrical devices of every kind. Anything an inventor might need was here.

The laboratory's greatest resource, however, was not its equipment but the men who helped Edison. Back in Newark, he had assembled a dedicated crew who joined him in Menlo Park. Among these men, Charles Batchelor and John Kruesi were probably the most talented. Batchelor, a native of Manchester, England, had learned the intricacies of machinery in the British textile mills; he had a

Edison (center, with straw hat on his lap) with his workers on the front steps of the Menlo Park laboratory.

patient, methodical manner that balanced Edison's more impetuous style. An accomplished draftsman, he could translate Edison's rough ideas into detailed drawings. The Swiss-born Kruesi, meanwhile, excelled at making things. Working from Edison's ideas and Batchelor's drawings, he turned them into finely crafted machines and instruments.

Although Edison was not yet 30 years old, he was known to his staff—affectionately—as "the old man." Following their boss's example, Edison's workers were a hard-driving bunch who put in long hours and took their jobs seriously. Yet they worked together in a spirit of good humor and loved to exchange stories and join in songfests during breaks in the busy routine. Since Menlo Park offered none of the amusements found in a city, the men had to amuse themselves.

Unfortunately, so did Mary Edison. If she had any hope that she would see more of her husband after the move to Menlo Park, she was disappointed. Occasionally, he took her to New York to see a play, but such evenings were rare. Although the laboratory was only a few hundred yards from the Edisons' house, the inventor became so immersed in his work that he often stayed at the lab for days at a time. He liked to experiment well into the night and take naps when he felt like it, curling up fully clothed on a pile of old newspapers. Though he loved Mary, he was more comfortable with the all-male world of his laboratory than with the young woman who had borne his children.

Those children now numbered two; Thomas Alva, Jr., had arrived in January. Edison nicknamed Marion "Dot" and her brother "Dash," after the signals in Morse code. He was fond of his children but only too happy to leave their upbringing to their mother—a trait he shared with many fathers of his day.

In addition to caring for the children, Mary busied herself by furnishing the five-bedroom house in lavish Victorian style. She filled it with expensive chairs, sofas, and rugs. Her taste for luxury extended even to her groceries, which she ordered from a New York store. Her husband, for his part, spared no expense when it came to equipping his laboratory. Thus, the Edisons' financial state remained precarious.

Much of Edison's income was now coming from Western Union. Although the dispute over the quadruplex was still thrashing around in the courts, Edison and the telegraph company had reached a separate agreement in 1875 for the development of an acoustic telegraph. Building on recent discoveries that musical tones could be sent over a wire by electricity, Edison was trying to see whether telegraphic signals could be split up into different sounds. He hoped that this might allow for the transmission of a greater number of messages than even the quadruplex could deliver.

There were two other freelance inventors at work on the problem of transmitting sounds by electricity: Elisha Gray of Chicago and Alexander Graham Bell of Boston. In January 1876 (while Edison was getting ready for the move to Menlo Park), Gray managed, with his version of the acoustic telegraph, to send eight messages over a single wire 200 miles long. But he and Bell, working separately, were already on the verge of something even more amazing. In February they both filed claims with the U.S. Patent Office for a device that could transmit the human voice over an electrified wire.

The proposed invention was, of course, the telephone. The patent office gave Bell's claim precedence over Gray's, and on March 10, Bell and his assistant, Thomas A. Watson, conducted one of the most famous experiments in scientific history. In Bell's Boston workshop, they wired a crude transmitter to a receiver in another room. With this apparatus, they hoped to convert the pattern of sound waves into a pattern of electrical current that would then be changed back into sound waves at the other end of the wire.

With his mouth close to the transmitter, Bell spoke.

"Mr. Watson," he said, "come here; I want to see you." Poised at the receiver, Watson could make out the words, faint but distinguishable.

The telephone caused a sensation, and over the next few months, Bell continued his experiments. By fall, he had the device working over a distance of several miles. It remained primitive, however. The sounds it transmitted could barely be heard.

Not to be outdone by Bell, Edison began telephone experiments of his own. By the spring of 1877, he and Batchelor had invented a receiver that could send the sounds of certain musical instruments blaring across a large room. Perfecting the transmitter presented a tougher prob-

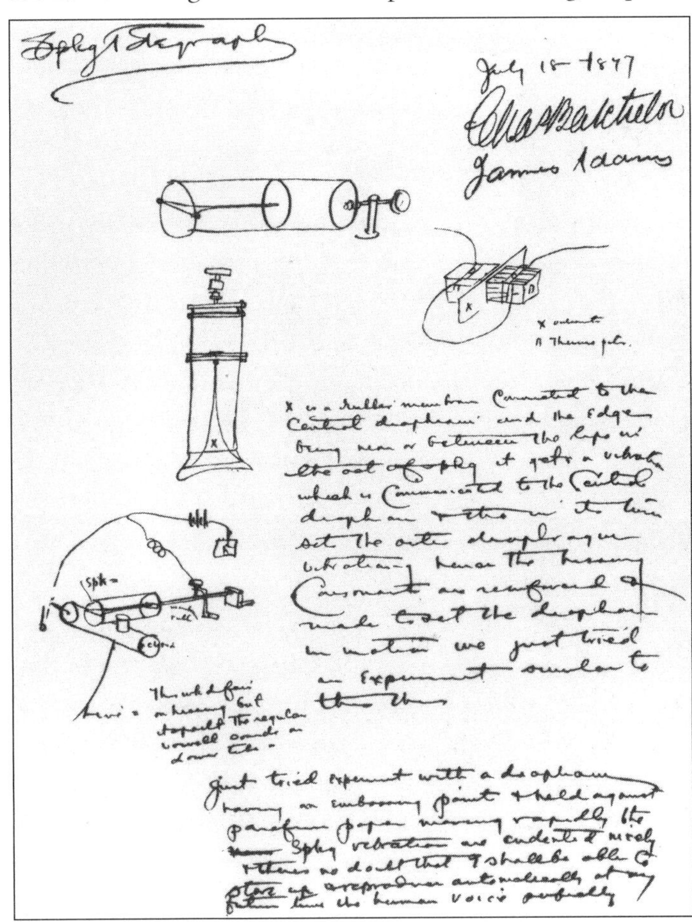

A page from Edison's notebook showing sketches he made relating to the telephone. Edison made crucial improvements in the telephone following the breakthrough experiments of Alexander Graham Bell.

lem, however. Though better than Bell's device, the early transmitters Edison and Batchelor produced still could not handle the finer articulations of the human voice.

Edison and Batchelor finally solved the problem of the troublesome transmitter with a simple carbon button. They found that when they formed a small disk from a mixture of rubber and carbon and then incorporated it into their transmitter, it improved the articulation tremendously.

But there was another problem. Officials at Western Union, Edison's main backer, were skeptical about the commercial potential of the telephone. When Bell had offered to sell them his patents for $100,000, they turned him down. They were even untroubled when Bell formed his own company. If the device turned out to have any value, they believed that Edison could come up with a version that would get around Bell's patents. But they were not certain that they even wanted whatever Edison might provide.

Thus, as Edison labored to improve the telephone's performance, he was also thinking about how he might make the device useful to Western Union. Since the company's main business was sending and delivering messages, he began to wonder if human speech, transmitted via telephone, could be recorded in some way and thus turned into a deliverable message. In these thoughts lay the seed of what was to be one of Edison's most celebrated inventions: the phonograph. Edison, without fully realizing it, was conceiving of a talking machine.

His experiments with the telephone had familiarized Edison with diaphragms—small, thin disks of metal or other material that vibrate in response to sound waves. One day he got the idea of attaching a pin to a diaphragm and placing a ribbon of wax paper beneath it. "I rigged up an instrument hastily and pulled a strip of paper through it, at the same time shouting 'Halloo!'" Edison recalled. "Then the paper was pulled through again so that its marks actuated the point of another diaphragm. My friend Batchelor and I listened breathlessly."

They heard a distinct sound, which, Edison said, "a strong imagination might have translated into the original 'Halloo.'" The experiment was hardly conclusive, but it inspired Edison to do further testing.

For several months, Edison worked with possible recording substances such as wax, chalk, and tinfoil. Word began to leak out from Menlo Park about a new machine that would somehow preserve telephone conversations. In early December Edison presented John Kruesi with some sketches and instructed him to build the device they illustrated. Kruesi wanted to know what it was for. "The machine must talk," said Edison.

With his usual craftsmanship (and some skepticism), Kruesi fashioned pieces of brass and iron into the machine Edison requested. Its central feature, once completed, was a small, rotating cylinder horizontally mounted on a baseboard. Two diaphragms, each with a needle (or stylus) attached, were fitted on opposite sides of the cylinder.

Edison's sketch for the original phonograph. Such sketches were recorded in laboratory notebooks as Edison developed his ideas for inventions.

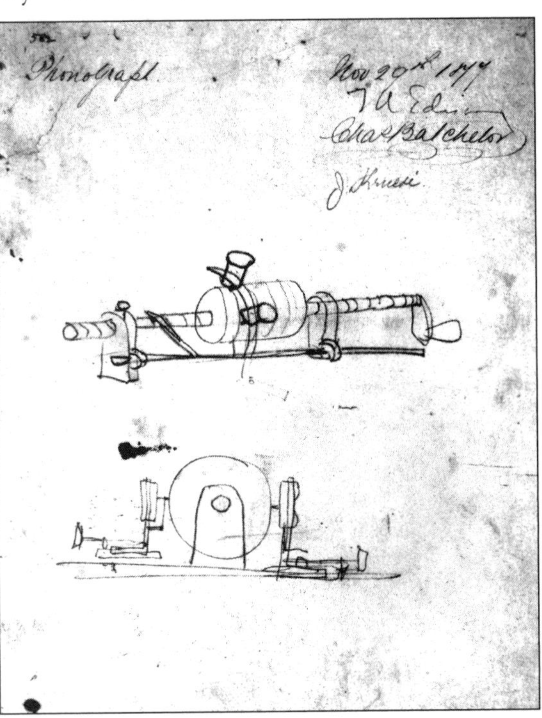

It was tested on the night of December 4, 1877. With his workers looking on, Edison carefully wrapped a sheet of tinfoil around the cylinder and lowered the needle of one of the diaphragms onto it. Turning a crank at one end of the cylinder, he shouted some words into the disk. According to most accounts, he recited the familiar nursery rhyme "Mary Had a Little Lamb."

Edison returned the cylinder to its starting point and placed the needle of the second diaphragm in the groove that had been impressed into the tinfoil. He turned the crank again, and to everyone's astonishment, the voice of Thomas Edison came forth. "I was never so taken aback in all my life," Edison later remembered. "I was always afraid of things that worked the first time."

Edison and his men stayed up the rest of the night, tinkering further with the phonograph to get better results. They sang and talked into it and were amazed when each time it reproduced a voice. When they were satisfied that it worked well enough, a second model of the phonograph was made for the patent office.

On December 7, Edison and Batchelor journeyed to New York and called on Alfred Beach, an editor of the magazine *Scientific American.* Placing the phonograph on his desk, Edison turned the crank. Beach was stunned by what he heard, and he later told his readers that "the machine inquired as to our health, asked how we liked the phonograph, informed us that *it* was very well, and bid us a cordial good night."

To listen to the talking machine, members of the *Scientific American* staff began crowding into Beach's office. Soon the editor was afraid the floor would collapse. The newspapers carried a story about Edison's remarkable new invention the next day.

Edison's name quickly became famous. He was hailed as "the wizard of Menlo Park," and the once-sleepy village witnessed a daily invasion of reporters, curiosity seekers, and scientists. Edison was asked to give public demonstrations of the phonograph, causing many observers to wonder whether the inventor was a ventriloquist.

The Reverend John Heyl Vincent, a prominent clergyman, came to Edison's lab to test the authenticity of the invention. He rapidly recited a series of hard-to-pronounce biblical names into the recording diaphragm; when the machine replayed them, the minister was convinced it was no trick. No one but himself, the Reverend Vincent said, could have spoken those names so quickly.

In April of 1878, Edison took the phonograph to Washington where he demonstrated it to members of Congress; to Joseph Henry, director of the Smithsonian Institution and the National Academy of Sciences; and, finally, to President Rutherford B. Hayes. The self-taught, plain-spoken inventor from the Midwest was now a folk hero—and one who was welcomed into the nation's highest circles.

Of all the many inventions Edison would complete during his lifetime, the phonograph remained his favorite, and it was certainly his most original. "This is my baby," he told a reporter, "and I expect it to grow up and be a big feller and support me in my old age."

Surprisingly, however, Edison did not exploit the invention's full potential right away. For years it would remain a primitive device, requiring great care and skill to operate properly. The tinfoil sheets could record for little more than a minute and wore out quickly, and the sound quality was still poor. Although Edison tinkered with some improvements—such as using wax as a recording substance—he did little in 1878 to take the device past the novelty stage. The Edison Speaking Phonograph Company, formed in January of that year to manufacture the machines, sold them mainly to showmen who arranged demonstrations for curious crowds.

The phonograph would, of course, become the foundation of the multibillion-dollar musical recording industry, but that was still years away. Edison himself predicted that its main use would be to record business dictation, yet he did not set out at once to develop it along those lines. Instead, he abandoned the device—temporarily—to become intensely involved in a new project. He was now on the verge of the most ambitious undertaking of his career.

THE PHONOGRAPH

In spite of his deafness—or perhaps because of it—Edison was fascinated by sound and acoustics. When he plunged into the development of his phonograph in 1877, he was already familiar with some of the prior research showing that each sound produced a distinctive shape. Twenty years earlier, a French inventor named Leon Scott had created a machine called a phonautograph, which used a hog bristle attached to a diaphragm to trace a wavy line from sound vibrations onto the carbon-coated surface of a rotating cylinder. Scott's device was clearly a forerunner of Edison's invention and even looked much like it.

As primitive as it was, Edison's first phonograph was quite ingenious. On the surface of the metal cylinder was inscribed a continuous groove in the shape of a helix. When a sheet of tinfoil was wrapped around the cylinder, the phonograph needle was placed so that it followed the groove underneath the foil. As Edison and his assistants shouted into the diaphragm, the sound vibrations indented the tinfoil into the cylinder groove, leaving a new groove in the tinfoil itself. The depth of the impression in the tinfoil changed with each new sound. This became known as a hill-and-dale recording because it involved variations in depth along the "floor" of the recording groove. In later versions of the Edison phonograph—after the inventor had switched to wax as a recording substance—the needle actually cut a groove into the record instead of simply impressing one. This technique greatly improved the sound quality. The recordings were still of the hill-and-dale type, however.

In the 1890s, a German named Emile Berliner devised a new method of recording using a flat disk instead of a cylinder. Its recording groove was in the shape of a spiral rather than a helix. And instead of hill-and-dale recordings, Berliner's machine made lateral recordings. This means that the sound variations were registered in the sides of the groove rather than its floor. If looked at under a magnifying glass, the groove resembled a wavy line.

By the 1930s, disk records became the single standard of the recording industry. The next major innovation came in the 1950s when stereophonic

The original phonograph was first tested successfully by Edison on December 4, 1877. The words of "Mary Had a Little Lamb" were the first words accurately repeated by the machine.

records were introduced. In this type of record, two separate soundtracks were recorded in a single groove, resulting in a sound more lifelike than ever before.

Today, with the popularity of recordings on cassette tapes and compact disks, the phonograph record is all but extinct. Yet the industry spawned by Edison's original invention is alive and well—an ongoing testament to the inventor's genius.

CHAPTER

6

The Electric Light

On April 1, 1878, the *New York Graphic* ran a story with the headline, "Edison Invents a Machine that Will Feed the Human Race." The story was an April Fool's joke, but Edison's "wizardry" was now so famous that to many, it did appear that he could do anything. Other newspapers picked up the *Graphic* story and ran it as straight news.

If the world thought that Edison could do anything, the inventor himself was probably not so sure. By late spring he was feeling sick and exhausted. Since inventing the phonograph six months earlier, he had given countless demonstrations of the machine. Although he relished public attention, he was starting to buckle under the strain.

Edison took a much-needed vacation in July. Professor George Barker of the University of Pennsylvania, who had arranged Edison's demonstration of the phonograph to the National Academy of Sciences, invited the inventor to join an expedition to the Rocky Mountains. The trip's purpose was to observe a total eclipse of the sun that was due to occur late that month.

Edison had recently invented a device he called a tasimeter, a kind of thermometer that was supposed to reg-

In 1878, Edison (far right, with arms folded) traveled to Rawlins, Wyoming, with a group of scientists to observe a solar eclipse. Edison used the eclipse to test his new tasimeter—a thermometer designed to register very small changes in temperature.

ister changes in temperature as small as one-millionth of a degree Fahrenheit. Edison planned to test it during the eclipse by using it to measure fluctuations in the sun's heat.

Although the tasimeter tests were inconclusive (and the device never gained practical use), Edison enjoyed the trip immensely. It lasted two months and took the inventor to such places as Wyoming, Nevada, Utah, and California. During one leg of the journey, Edison rode on the "cowcatcher," the iron grille at the very front of the locomotive, where he had an unobstructed view of the magnificent western scenery. There was also plenty of hunting, fishing, and campfire chat. By August 26, Edison was back in Menlo Park, refreshed and ready to resume work.

The trip stimulated Edison's inventive imagination. As Batchelor recalled, his boss returned to the lab full of ideas "for using the power of the falls [waterfalls] for electricity & utilizing it in the mines for drills etc." Edison was also eager to visit William Wallace's brass and copper foundry in Ansonia, Connecticut. From Professor Barker he had learned about a marvelous system of electric lighting that Wallace was using at his factory. Accompanied by a *New York Sun* reporter, Edison and Batchelor went to Ansonia on September 8.

Edison was impressed by what he saw. Wallace, who shared Edison's fascination with electricity, had been building generators of the dynamo type for several years. Recently Wallace had linked one of his machines to a water-driven turbine at a stream near his foundry. The dynamo produced an electric current far more powerful than any produced by the chemical reactions in the batteries Edison was accustomed to using. Its two main components were an electromagnet and a wire-coil assembly called an armature. When the turbine rotated the armature within the magnet's field, a current was created and channeled into a circuit that Wallace had linked to the foundry a quarter-mile away.

At the foundry, the electric current powered a series of arc lights, which at that time represented the only kind of electric lighting to have any practical use. In an arc light, a strong current actually "jumps" across a small gap between two plates or rods made of carbon. The result is a brilliant light equal to the power of thousands of candles.

As the *Sun* reporter wrote, witnessing Wallace's light-and-power system "filled up Mr. Edison's cup of joy. He ran from the instruments to the lights, and from the lights back to the instrument. . . . He calculated the power of the instrument and of the lights, the probable loss of power in transmission, the amount of coal the instrument would save in a day, a week, a month, a year, and the result of such saving on manufacturing."

Ideas were racing through Edison's mind like wildfire. The possibilities of using electricity as an all-purpose power source excited him endlessly. At the same time, he was sure that he could create a type of electric lamp that would be far more useful than the arc light.

Arc lights were fine for large spaces such as Wallace's foundry. Some were already being used to light streets in Europe. But what intrigued Edison was the idea of inventing a lamp that could be used in small spaces such as homes and offices. Its illumination would have to be much softer than the blinding light produced by arc systems.

More than a dozen inventors before Edison had tried, with little success, to create just such a light. In the early 1800s, the English scientist Sir Humphry Davy had shown that when electric current flows through certain materials, they become incandescent, or start to glow. Yet inventors who tried to use this principle to create a practical lamp all failed. Their devices often worked for a few minutes, but inevitably the incandescent material melted or burned up.

It was a perplexing problem, and on and off over the years, Edison had even tried a few electric-light experiments of his own. He had performed the most recent ones during the fall of 1877 but set them aside when the phonograph began to demand his full attention.

The visit to Wallace's foundry convinced Edison to take up those experiments again and to create a practical incandescent lamp. In a matter of days, he became convinced that a major breakthrough was imminent. Edison ordered one of Wallace's dynamos for his laboratory and drafted his first electric-light proposal for the patent office.

By mid-September, Edison was so confident his ideas would work that he notified the press. Summoning a *New York Sun* reporter, he explained how he planned to use Wallace's dynamos to light lower Manhattan. It was a grand scheme he envisioned, one that included not only inventing the lamp itself but devising an entire system of electrical distribution.

At that time, major cities like New York used gaslighting systems, and it was on these that Edison planned to model his electrical system. In place of the underground pipes that carried gas into buildings, Edison would use underground cables for conducting electricity. Inside homes and offices, Edison told the *Sun* reporter, existing gas fixtures could be easily converted into electrical fixtures. And like gas, the inventor predicted, electrical consumption could be measured on meters and the customers billed accordingly.

A key to the system as Edison saw it was the parallel circuit. Arc lights were usually wired in series, which meant that if one light burned out, the entire circuit was broken. In a parallel circuit, however, smaller lines branch off from the main one, supplying each lamp fixture independently. That way one lamp can be switched on and off without affecting any of the other lamps.

Despite his optimism, Edison was still a long way from accomplishing what he hoped. But his boasts in the newspapers created a stir within the financial world. Western Union officials, along with other potential investors, were attracted by Edison's claims, and discussions about forming a company to back his electric-light experiments soon began in New York. The Edison Electric Light Company, incorporated in November, was the result of those talks.

Representing Edison in the negotiations was Grosvenor P. Lowrey, a New York attorney who also worked for Western Union. As Edison's work proceeded, it became Lowrey's responsibility to keep the ever-nervous moneymen from becoming too nervous and withdrawing their support. Lowrey was good at his job, and when the money began to run out, he pulled in additional investors. The most important were the banking partners Anthony Drexel and J. Pierpont Morgan.

Edison had barely plunged into the electric-light experiments when he realized what a thorny task he had taken on. The optimism at Menlo Park seesawed considerably over the next year, but through it all Edison remained stubbornly persistent.

"The electric light," Edison said later, "has caused me the greatest amount of study and has required the most elaborate experiments. I was never myself discouraged, or inclined to be hopeless of success. I cannot say the same for all my associates."

Of the many problems to be solved, finding the right material for the incandescent element, which came to be called the filament, was probably the toughest. Edison and his men tried dozens of substances—carbon, chromium, steel, gold, boron, iridium, to name only a few—and fashioned them into a variety of shapes, lengths, and thicknesses.

For months platinum was the favored material, but it had major drawbacks. Aside from being a rare metal and

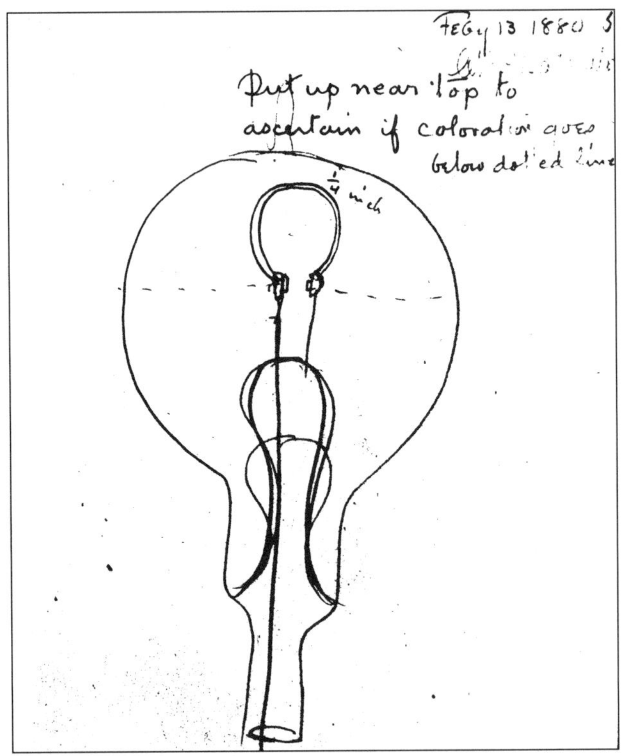

On February 13, 1880, Edison sketched this lightbulb in his notebook.

thus extremely expensive, it melted at the high temperatures needed for incandescence. To keep the filament from melting, Edison's early lamp designs included regulating devices that were designed to break the electric circuit when the filament began to overheat and then restore the circuit as the filament cooled. Yet the regulators were overly complicated and themselves full of "bugs." The power source presented another obstacle. After deciding that Wallace's generator was unsuitable for his purposes, Edison purchased other dynamos, none of which gave him the results he wanted. Thus, inventing a better generator became an important part of the busy activity at the lab.

The experimenting was haphazard at first, but Edison and his men were, after all, breaking new ground. Although others had tried to invent an incandescent light, none had conceived of a system as elaborate and ambitious as the one that was taking shape in Menlo Park. Through trial and error, the Edison team gradually gained a better understanding of what they were doing, and the work became more systematic.

Bit by bit, they made discoveries and reached conclusions that would bring them ever closer to a successful invention. About three months into the experiments, they crossed one of the most important hurdles when Edison determined that the lamp should be of high resistance.

In electrical science, resistance refers to the properties of a substance that restrict the flow of electricity. In a wire, for example, the length, thickness, and conductivity of the material from which it is made all affect its resistance. If a wire is long, thin, and made from a relatively poor conductor, it is said to have high resistance. On the other hand, a short, thick wire made from a good conducting material has low resistance.

Previous inventors had experimented with low-resistance lamps, but Edison saw that these would never work in the large-scale lighting system that he envisioned. For such a system to operate efficiently and economically, Edison found, each lamp should use only a tiny portion of the current. A low-resistance system would require an enormous amount of current, along with a huge amount of copper in the main cable, to service lamps at the farthest reaches of the circuit. With a high resistance system, Edison saw that both the current and the copper needed for lighting many lamps over long distances could be greatly reduced. This meant that he could make electric lighting competitive in cost with gaslighting.

Another important conclusion Edison reached was the need for creating a vacuum around the filament. He had discovered that gases trapped inside the pores of the platinum filament were released when the current was turned on. If he could get rid of those gases and the surrounding air by sealing the filament in a glass bulb and pumping the air out, Edison thought he might be able to improve the performance of the platinum.

Once he decided that a vacuum was necessary, Edison searched for the best vacuum pumps then available. By the spring of 1879, he had bought two such devices, called Geissler pumps, and soon afterward he acquired an even better device called a Sprengel pump. Edison studied the pumps carefully and made his own improvements in them.

An illustration from the October 18, 1879 issue of Scientific American *shows Edison's first generator, which his workers nicknamed the "long-legged Mary Ann." The nickname was suggested by the two iron poles that formed the magnet of the generator.*

As the electric-light experiments progressed, Edison not only acquired new equipment but added new workers to his team, which now numbered about 25. Among the most valuable was Francis R. Upton, a Bowdoin College graduate who had studied advanced physics at Princeton

University and in Berlin, Germany. Initially recruited to research all the previous work done on the electric light, Upton had the best grasp of scientific theory of anyone at Menlo Park.

Early in 1879, Upton was put to work on the generator problem, and it was largely thanks to his efforts that a better dynamo was constructed. The men nicknamed the new machine the "long-legged Mary Ann" because of the two iron poles, four and a half feet high, that formed its magnet. The rotating armature, consisting of a hollow cylinder wrapped in copper wire, was placed at the base of the machine between the two poles. A steam engine, linked to the dynamo by belts and pulleys, was used to rotate the armature.

The Mary Ann was the most advanced generator of its day. Whereas earlier dynamos were only about 60 percent efficient, the Mary Ann achieved more than 80 percent efficiency. It was a major triumph for the Edison lab, but no one stopped to rest. There was still too much to do.

As the months went by, the filament material remained the most vexing problem, even though Edison kept a stubborn faith in platinum. Using a vacuum did appear to improve the metal's performance: the lamps shone brighter and lasted longer. To help with the vacuum experiments, Edison hired a 20-year-old glass blower named Ludwig Boehm, who had recently come to the United States from Germany. Because the delicate pumps were made largely of glass, it became Boehm's job to keep them in good repair and to carry out Edison's ideas for improving the devices. Boehm also fashioned the glass bulbs that were being used to enclose the filaments of the lamps. His expertise proved critical, for by the end of the summer the experiments were yielding near-perfect vacuums.

Edison's designs for the lamp were now much simpler. By autumn he had finally decided to eliminate the complicated regulators, which had caused nothing but headaches.

He was close to having a workable design, if he could only solve the filament problem. Despite the recent improvements, the platinum lamps still burned for only a few hours at most.

Equally frustrating was the resistance of the platinum, which was much too low to meet Edison's requirements. Seeking to increase its resistance, Edison's men experimented with dozens of shapes for the filament. They tried to keep the wire as thin as possible and to maximize its length by twisting it into tight spirals. Yet the metal was simply too good a conductor, and the efforts to raise its resistance to Edison's standards failed.

Even if the physical properties of platinum had made it an ideal filament material, it had still another drawback that Edison could not solve: its cost. Platinum sold for $12 an ounce, and Upton calculated that a single platinum-filament lamp would cost $98! With typical optimism, Edison bought maps of mining regions and made inquiries to miners and prospectors around the world. He hoped to discover that platinum was not as rare a metal as everyone believed. Later, in an imaginative mood, he declared that the sand of the Pacific coast beaches was loaded with platinum particles and that he could invent an ore separator capable of supplying all the platinum they needed. Edison's hopes for finding a bountiful platinum supply were a fantasy, but he continued using the metal as a filament material well into the fall.

The electric-light experiments had now gone on for a year. As intense as they were, they did not make up the only activity at Menlo Park. Work continued on the telephone, and negotiations were underway in London to set up a British telephone company using Edison's patents.

Among those Edison had sent across the Atlantic to assist in the negotiations was his own nephew Charley, the 19-year-old son of his brother Pitt. A gifted inventor in his own right, Charley was mainly responsible for devising a new telephone receiver that Edison was promoting along with his own carbon-button transmitter.

In October, news arrived that Charley was seriously ill in Paris. He was not expected to live. For 40 hours, beginning on October 17, work at Menlo Park stopped while the men held a death watch. On October 19, a telegram announced that Charley had died the day before. Edison arranged for his nephew's body to be brought back to the United States for burial at Port Huron.

Sadly, the news of Charley's death came on the eve of one of Edison's greatest triumphs: finding the right filament material. After all the experimentation with costly platinum, the proper substance turned out to be something quite cheap and readily available. It was carbon.

Because of the telephone experiments, carbon was familiar stuff at Menlo Park. It was easily obtainable as lampblack, a thin residue left on the inside of an oil lamp's glass chimney. Legend has it that Edison was pondering his experiments one night when he began idly rolling a piece of compressed lampblack between his fingers. Noticing that he had formed a thin thread of carbon, Edison supposedly realized at that moment that the element might make a good filament material.

In truth, many of Edison's predecessors had used carbon in their electric-light experiments, and it was one of the substances tried—and rejected—during the early stages of the Menlo Park research. But in October 1879, for whatever reason, experiments with carbon resumed.

In the earlier experiments, Edison had ruled out carbon because it burned up too easily. But since that time, while struggling to get the platinum filaments to work, the inventor and his team had obtained near-perfect vacuums in sealed glass bulbs. If carbon was placed in a vacuum, they realized, it would not burn up because the oxygen neces-

text continues on page 80

THE ELECTRIC LIGHT THEN AND NOW

In its essential components, today's electric light bulb is much like the one Edison invented in 1879. It includes a glass bulb and a thin filament that becomes incandescent when an electric current is passed through it. There are several key differences, however.

Edison used a filament made of carbon. Today's bulbs use filaments made from a metal called tungsten. It is interesting to note that tungsten was one of the elements with which Edison experimented when he was trying to find the right filament material for his light. Unfortunately, tungsten is an extremely hard element, and it proved too difficult to shape with the tools available to Edison at the time. It was only in the early 1900s that methods were developed for drawing tungsten through dies (special devices used for shaping and cutting metals) and forming it into a thin wire.

Whereas the Edison light bulb surrounded the filament with a vacuum, today's bulbs contain gases, usually a mixture of nitrogen and argon. These gases, which do not interact chemically with the tungsten, help to slow down the vaporization of the filament and thus lengthen the life of the bulb. The typical light bulb of today can last for about a thousand hours.

For many years, light bulbs were made from clear glass. Around 1925, however, manufacturers developed a process for frosting bulbs by treating the inside surface of the glass with hydrofluoric acid. The frosting reduces the glare from the filament.

What happens when an electric light is switched on? In other words, how does the filament become incandescent, or light up? In the 1800s, scientists knew only that incandescence occurred—they could not really say how it happened. Today, as with most of the principles of electricity and electronics, incandescence can be explained by the behavior of electrons.

When the electric current heats the lamp filament to a high enough temperature (4,500 degrees Fahrenheit in a tungsten lamp), some of the electrons in the filament atoms absorb additional energy and move away from their usual orbits around the nuclei of the atoms. But, almost instantaneously, they drop back to their regular orbits, and as they fall, their excess energy is released in the form of photons—the fundamental units of visible light. When we observe an electric light in use, we are witnessing the continual release of billions of photons.

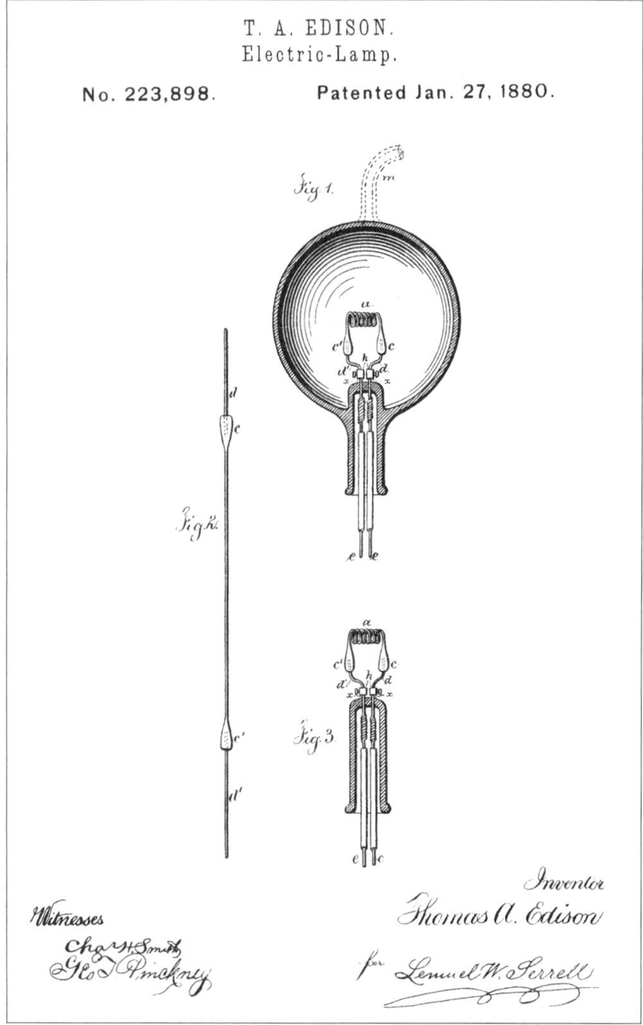

The patent drawing for Edison's electric lamp. Interestingly, the diagram shows the filament in the form of a spiral. The actual lamp produced by Edison used a horseshoe-shaped filament.

text continued from page 77

sary for combustion would be absent. October 21, 1879, is usually given as the date of the first successful carbon-lamp experiments. Edison's lab records, however, show that it was actually on October 22 that the first truly promising results occurred. In his notes, Charles Batchelor recorded a series of experiments using various types of carbon filaments. He took materials such as soft paper, fishing line, and cardboard and baked them in an oven. This left them charred, or carbonized.

In each case, the brittle filament was carefully fitted into a lamp circuit, and the air was pumped out of the bulb. Then the current, supplied by a series of batteries, was turned on. The best results came from a simple piece of carbonized cotton thread. It glowed dimly at first but grew brighter as the power was increased. The lamp worked for nearly 15 hours and ultimately gave off a light equal to 30 candles. Best of all, the resistance of carbon matched Edison's requirements.

At long last, Edison and his men knew that they were on the right track. In early November, Edison applied for a patent for the carbon-filament lamp. Over the next few weeks, he conducted experiments with a variety of carbonized materials, including all sorts of wood shavings and papers. A horseshoe-shaped piece of carbonized cardboard seemed to work best. The pace at Menlo Park became frenetic as Edison's team raced to perfect the lamp and turn it into a mass-producible product.

During the long year of experimentation, Edison's investors had often feared that they were pouring their money down the drain. Each time that their fears neared the breaking point, Grosvenor Lowrey had to step in and reassure them. Now, as word of Edison's success began to spread, the financiers pressed the inventor for a public exhibition of the light. This would help build the momentum needed for the next step: launching an electrical lighting system.

The demonstration was planned for New Year's Eve, and Edison's team wasted no time in getting it ready. A small-scale system was rapidly assembled at Menlo Park using the Mary Ann generators and more than 50 lamps. On December 21, the *New York Herald* ran a story headlined "The Great Inventor's Triumph in Electric Illumination," describing in detail the arduous history of the invention. As a result, visitors began to flock to Menlo Park even before the exhibition was ready.

When New Year's Eve finally came, Edison could not have hoped for a more successful demonstration. Along with a new year and a new decade, the electric age had also begun.

Generators inside the Pearl Street Station in New York City, where Edison launched his successful light-and-power system in 1882.

CHAPTER

7

Building a System

Among the visitors who were awestruck by the New Year's Eve demonstration at Menlo Park was Henry Villard, head of the Oregon Railway and Navigation Company and one of the investors in the Edison Electric Light Company. Early in 1880, he approached the inventor about installing a lighting system on board his new steamship, the *Columbia*, which was then being outfitted at a New York dock.

After giving Villard's proposal some thought, Edison decided that an electric light installation on the *Columbia* would bring good publicity. He put Francis Upton in charge of the project, which was carried out that spring. Four Mary Ann generators were placed on the ship, along with 150 lamps. The system was tested on April 28, and on May 9, the ship left New York for Portland, Oregon. As the *Columbia* cruised southward to round the tip of South America and then head north, its lighting system brought delight and astonishment in every port at which it stopped.

The success of the *Columbia* installation pleased Edison, for it showed the world the practicality of his light. But he considered it a small triumph. His primary aim was still to create a full-scale urban lighting system, and achieving that goal made the laboratory a site of extraordinary activity in 1880. The size of Edison's work force swelled to nearly 65 men. The inventor also acquired an old factory building near the laboratory to convert into a lamp factory.

The activity was divided into several key tasks. Improving the lamp was still a top priority, and the search continued for an even better filament material. By summer, carbonized bamboo fiber was the favored choice. More durable and easier to handle than carbonized cardboard, bamboo gave the best results yet seen at Menlo Park.

Manufacturing the lights on a large scale posed new problems. The experimental lamps had been made from handblown glass bulbs, but now bulbs were needed by the hundreds. After some unsuccessful attempts to mass-produce bulbs from molds, Edison made arrangements with the Corning Glass Works to have the fragile globes made to order.

In order to have enough lamps to operate his system, Edison knew that he would have to find a way to mass-produce them. Here, workers stand in front of the Menlo Park lamp factory, which began operation in October 1880.

The vacuum pumps also had to be adapted to factory-style production. In the laboratory, operating the pumps required great skill and hours of close tending. Using a small electric motor, Edison found a way of partially mechanizing the pumps so that they worked faster and did not need as much human attention. This marked one of the first instances in which electrically driven machinery was introduced into the workings of a factory.

Many of the lamp problems were minute but still worrisome. The filament clamps were one example. Although Edison had long since abandoned platinum as a filament material, the expensive metal was still being used to make the clamps that attached the lead-in wires to the carbon filament. Nickel clamps were later substituted, but they were hard to make. Finally, one of Edison's chemists devised a cheap and easy way to plate the wires directly to the ends of the filament.

Even the lamp sockets were a challenge. The earliest designs consisted of wooden sockets with copper contact strips inside. These were adequate for upright lamps but posed problems for ceiling-mounted lamps because the bulbs could not be firmly secured. Eventually, Edison introduced screw-type mountings made of plaster of Paris, resulting in bulbs that were quite similar in appearance to their modern descendants.

Unlike the lamps, improving the dynamo was not a concern at first. Edison believed that the Mary Ann generators, each of which could light about 60 lamps, would be adequate for any system. He soon revised his thinking, however, in favor of a more powerful dynamo that could handle up to a thousand lamps. Construction of a prototype machine began late in the year.

Yet another task during 1880 was devising the system of conductors that would carry the electric current from the generators to the lights. For the hastily arranged demonstration on New Year's Eve, Edison had used overhead wires strung from poles. The inventor knew from his telegraph experience, however, that such wires were vulnerable to the weather. In Edison's view, the best solution was the use of underground cables, modeled after the underground pipes used for gaslighting and water systems.

Thus, in preparation for a new demonstration system at Menlo Park, Edison's men began digging trenches and laying cables outside the laboratory during the spring of 1880. The biggest challenge here was creating an insulation to protect the wires. Upton and several others experimented with a variety of materials and combinations of materials. They finally settled on an insulation that required wrapping the wires in layers of muslin and applying a smelly coating of tar, paraffin, linseed oil, and asphalt.

Even with all the preparations for the light-and-power system, Edison found time for other inventions. At about the same time the experimental underground cables were being laid, Edison workers were also laying some narrow-gauge railroad tracks in a nearby field. The rails eventually encircled a small hill, covering a total distance of a third of a mile.

Soon they placed a six-foot electric locomotive on the tracks. Its motor was an adapted Mary Ann generator laid on its side and mounted atop a four-wheel truck. An overturned beer crate served as the driver's seat, and a small passenger truck was coupled behind the little engine. The rails were wired to a pair of dynamos, which supplied power to the motor, and the locomotive could manage speeds up to 40 miles an hour.

Riding the little train required some bravery. Grosvenor Lowrey recalled one demonstration in which he was a passenger and John Kruesi was the driver: "The train jumped the track on a short curve, throwing Kruesi . . . face down in the dirt, and another man in a comical somersault through some underbrush."

Edison thought it was all great fun, but Kruesi did not agree. "Kruesi got up, his face bleeding and a good deal shaken," Lowrey remembered. "I shall never forget the expression of voice and face in which he said, with some foreign accent: 'Oh! Yes, pairfeckly safe!'"

Edison's electric locomotive was the first such machine built in America, and it might have been counted among his great achievements. Yet, even though he built a larger and more sophisticated locomotive in 1882 and would take on a few electric-train experiments several years after that, he never developed the invention to the extent that he might have. After rival inventors entered the field, Edison pretty much left it to them. Yet Edison's work laid the foundations for the streetcar and subway systems that later were built in many of the nation's major cities.

Edison might have spent more time on the train if he had not been struggling to launch the lighting system. As 1880 drew to a close, new public demonstrations, even more elaborate than the one of the year before, were

While working on his electric light system, Edison still found time to work on other projects, such as this electric railroad on the grounds of the Menlo Park facility.

planned at Menlo Park. Edison needed to show off the refinements in his system before he could begin installing it in an actual city.

From the start, it was taken for granted that the first urban electric-lighting system should be set up in a New York City neighborhood. To be economically feasible, Edison's calculations showed, the system should be installed in a small area with a high level of usage. New York fit that requirement perfectly. The city was also a good choice because most of Edison's investors were based there, and it was the New York press that had given him his greatest publicity.

Of course, installing such a system in New York meant that Edison had to convince city officials that it would work efficiently and safely. Otherwise, they would not permit the major disruptions that ripping up streets and installing cables would cause. In December, therefore, Edison invited members of the New York City Board of Aldermen to Menlo Park to inspect the system.

Edison treated the aldermen, along with other city officials and several directors of the Edison Electric Light Company, to a fine dinner with champagne. Describing the event, one newspaper headline read: "ALDERMEN AT MENLO PARK . . . The City Fathers Partake of a Collation, Swallow Innumerable Bumpers and Make the Most Scintillating Speeches."

The inventor's "wine-and-dine" tactics were a good complement to the technical demonstration, which now featured a stunning array of 400 lamps. The city officials left Menlo Park convinced that the power-and-light system would perform as advertised. Within a few months, the board of aldermen would grant Edison a franchise to install his system.

The December exhibitions drew other noted figures to the New Jersey laboratory as well. Sarah Bernhardt, the world-famous French actress, took time out from her

American tour to call on Edison. Even Jay Gould, the wily financier whom Edison was suing in connection with the quadruplex dispute (and who would soon take control of Western Union), came by for a look.

As 1881 rolled around, Edison began shifting his operations to New York. In February, he leased a mansion at 65 Fifth Avenue, which became the headquarters for overseeing the lighting system's installation. Arriving at his fine new building, the 34-year-old inventor reflected briefly on his phenomenal rags-to-riches rise. "We're up in the world now!" he told a reporter. "I remember ten years ago—I had just come from Boston—I had to walk the streets of New York all night because I hadn't the price of a bed. And now think of it! I'm going to occupy a whole house on Fifth Avenue."

Edison's return to New York came not a moment too soon, for the electric-lighting field was starting to draw competition. Most of these competitors were involved in arc-lighting systems. The Brush Company, for example, had installed arc lights in December 1880 along Broadway between 14th and 34th Streets. (This gave rise to Broadway's nickname, "The Great White Way.") However, there was one competitor, Hiram Maxim, who was promoting an incandescent system of his own. Maxim had installed incandescent lamps at the Mercantile Safe Deposit Company, a bank housed in the Equitable Building. Edison discounted Maxim's lamp as a mere copy of his cardboard-filament bulb—which it was—but it helped convince the inventor that he needed to launch his system as quickly as possible.

Although Edison had boasted more than two years earlier about creating a system that would light all of lower Manhattan, his claims were overly optimistic. The system he now had underway was less grand, covering only about 10 square blocks on the city's Lower East Side. Its boundaries were, on the east, the East River; on the west, the middle line of Nassau Street; on the north, the middle line of Spruce Street; and on the south, the middle line of Wall Street. Although the First District (as the area to be wired and lighted was called) did not quite match the inventor's original dream, it was still a remarkable start, and certainly more ambitious than anything his rivals were attempting.

Edison began moving equipment from Menlo Park to New York. The lab's machine shop, for example, was completely dismantled, and a new shop, christened the Edison Machine Works, was installed at 104 Goerck Street. Charles Dean, formerly Kruesi's chief assistant, was put in charge of the operation, which was to manufacture the powerful new dynamos needed for the system.

In order to supply electricity from Edison's Pearl Street station directly to individual offices and apartments, workers had to lay cables under the streets of New York City.

For his part, Kruesi headed the newly formed Edison Electric Tube Company at 65 Washington Street. It was faced with what was probably the most daunting task of all: digging the trenches and laying 15 miles of underground conductor cables. First the cables were fed into iron pipes, which were laid along the bottom of the trenches. Then the insulating mixture was poured into the pipes, where it surrounded the cables and was allowed to harden. Finally the trenches were refilled and the streets restored. Installing the conductors would require nearly 15 months to complete. Most of the work was done at night to minimize disruptions to those who lived and worked in the neighborhood.

To manufacture the various small appliances needed for the system—fixtures, lamp sockets, switches, and, later, meters for measuring electrical usage—Edison turned to the shop of Johann Sigmund Bergmann. A German-born craftsman who specialized in electrical devices, Bergmann had helped Edison manufacture many of his earlier inventions, including the phonograph. Edison now provided Bergmann with capital to expand his operations, which soon joined Edison's family of companies.

Back in Menlo Park, meanwhile, Francis Upton took charge of the lamp factory. He replaced Charles Batchelor, who had crossed the Atlantic to prepare exhibitions of the lighting system in London and Paris. Although the initial plan was to keep the lamp factory at Menlo Park, Edison decided later that year to move it into a much larger space in East Newark (now Harrison), New Jersey.

The era of Menlo Park, which represented the most amazing spurt of inventive energy in American history, was fast drawing to a close. The lab continued to serve as an experimental and testing center, but soon the various new shops in Manhattan had their own testing facilities. Edison maintained his house in the New Jersey village, although his family now divided much of its time between visits to Florida and the seashores of New York and New Jersey.

The site of the central power station for the First District was chosen by mid-spring of 1881. Edison purchased two adjacent buildings on Pearl Street, near the center of the district, and began adapting them to his needs. One building, at 257 Pearl Street, housed the dynamos, steam engines, and boilers. To bear the weight of all the heavy machinery, the structure had to be reinforced with wrought-iron supports. The building next door, at 255 Pearl Street, contained offices, storage space, sleeping quarters for the station operators, and testing facilities.

The dynamos Edison was having built at the machine works were much larger than the Mary Anns. Not only did Edison plan to use them in the Pearl Street station, but he wanted to send one of them, a 30-ton monstrosity that featured a radically new armature design, to the Paris Electrical Exhibition. The machine works crew labored through the summer preparing the dynamo and finally completed it in the early fall. After some last-minute tests, it was quickly disassembled, crated up, and shipped to France. Nicknamed Jumbo, after a famous circus elephant, it was the biggest electrical generator ever built and, along with the Edison light, won top honors in Paris. Edison's system completely overshadowed the work of his rivals at the exhibition, including Hiram Maxim and a British inventor named Joseph Swan, who had earlier completed a version of the incandescent light at almost the same time as Edison.

A second Jumbo, even bigger than the first, was soon sent to London to be used in a model lighting system that Edison's men were installing along the Holborn Viaduct, an elevated roadway in the city's financial district. This installation, though much less ambitious than the one underway in New York, offered an impressive demonstration of the Edison system. Stretching from Holborn Circus to the General Post Office a half mile away, it featured nearly a

text continues on page 96

MYSTERIOUS DISCOVERIES: ETHERIC FORCE AND THE EDISON EFFECT

As a practical inventor who often spoke disdainfully about theoretical science, Edison cared little about pursuing scientific knowledge for its own sake. During the course of his experiments, however, he sometimes stumbled across phenomena that would prove to be of great interest to "pure" scientists.

One such discovery occurred in November 1875, when Edison was conducting experiments with a vibrating magnet as part of his efforts to develop an acoustic telegraph. As he wrote in his lab notebooks, he observed some "particularly bright, scintillating sparks issuing from the core of the magnet." Experimenting further, Edison concluded that the sparks were unlike any other electrical occurrence he had seen. His instruments detected no electrical charge in the sparks, which could also pass through insulating materials such as glass and rubber. Deciding that the sparks must be "nonelectric," Edison called them "etheric force." (Etheric, as Edison used the term, referred to occurrences associated with the air or the heavens.)

Many scientists ridiculed Edison's claims that he had found something new, although one noted physicist, Dr. George M. Beard, believed that Edison had made a real discovery. Beard speculated that the sparks were "a radiant force, somewhere between light and heat on the one hand and magnetism and electricity on the other." Beard was not far off, for it is now apparent that what Edison observed was a form of high-frequency electromagnetic waves. (Electromagnetic waves, which have both electrical and magnetic components, include a whole range of radiations, such as visible light, ultraviolet light, radio waves, and X rays.)

Edison's etheric force was not really a new discovery. Years before, scientists such as Michael Faraday, Joseph Henry, and James Clerk Maxwell had either observed such phenomena or theorized about their existence. Yet no one seemed to make any connections between Edison's experiments and this earlier research. Another decade passed

MYSTERIOUS DISCOVERIES: ETHERIC FORCE AND THE EDISON EFFECT

text continued from page 93

In 1918, Edison stands next to his workbench holding the bulb he used in 1883 to demonstrate the "Edison effect."

before the findings of Edison and his predecessors came into sharper focus with the experiments of the German physicist Heinrich Rudolf Hertz. Between 1885 and 1889, Hertz conducted experiments confirming the existence of electromagnetic waves and became the first scientist to produce and detect radio waves. While etheric force intrigued Edison at first, he quickly forgot about it. His telegraph experiments and his upcoming move to Menlo Park were uppermost in his mind at the time. He would have a similar response a few years later to another accidental discovery—a finding that is now considered Edison's one authentic contribution to pure science.

This discovery came as an accident while Edison was trying to perfect his electric lamp during the early 1880s. He noticed that a blackish deposit kept appearing on the inside of his bulbs. Somehow, the inventor reasoned, carbon particles were being electrically conducted from the filament to the surface of the glass bulb. But how, he wondered, could this happen across a vacuum?

Investigating the mystery in 1883, Edison inserted a small platinum plate inside one of his bulbs, near the filament. With the aid of a meter for measuring current, he found that electricity did indeed flow between the filament and the metal plate of the electrode—without a wire connecting them!

Edison created and patented a special lamp to demonstrate the phenomenon, which came to be known as the Edison effect, or thermionic emission. But no one knew what to make of the discovery at the time, and Edison, just as he had done with etheric force, quickly abandoned his experiments and moved on to other things.

Scientists who investigated the Edison effect years later found that it was caused by the generation and movement of free electrons in space. The effect would, in the 20th century, form the basis of many of the electronic instruments used in radio, sound amplification, television, and radar. Like etheric force, the Edison effect hinted at a world still to be discovered. Yet, at the time Edison observed them, such phenomena were mere curiosities.

Edison was still alive when the electronic age finally came. Yet, oddly enough, he never developed much affection for electronic devices. When radio began to gain popularity during the 1920s, Edison predicted that it would be only a passing fad. One reason for Edison's resistance to this new technology was his poor hearing. The sound of early radios was filled with hisses and crackles, and bad as it was, it sounded even worse to someone with Edison's hearing problems.

text continued from page 92

thousand lamps that lit up the streets, shops, restaurants, hotels, and offices.

Edison's light-and-power system was also a hit at a London exhibition held at the Crystal Palace early in 1882. Using 12 Mary Ann generators, this demonstration repeated the success of the Paris exhibit and, along with the Holborn Viaduct station, amazed the British public. Edison's inventions were now truly an international sensation.

At about the same time as the London successes, the installation in New York met with a two-month delay, not for technical reasons but for personal ones. Mary Edison was not well, and her husband decided to take a break to look after her. Mary's poor health dated from the birth of her third child, Will, in 1878. Depressed by her husband's neglect, she stuffed herself with chocolates and so put on considerable weight. In February 1882, Edison took Mary to Florida, one of her favorite vacation spots. By April, her condition had improved, and Edison was back in New York.

Even as he raced to finish the First District installation, Edison found himself besieged with requests for "isolated systems" like the one he had placed aboard Henry Villard's *Columbia* in 1880. He had resisted at first, since he considered the creation of a large-scale system to be his main priority. Gradually, however, he succumbed to the pressure, and starting in 1881, he began to produce small systems that could light individual factories, stores, offices, and public buildings. Late in 1881, the Edison Company for Isolated Lighting was formed, and by the middle of 1882, nearly a hundred isolated plants were in use in the United States and Europe. Among those who purchased such plants were two of Edison's most prominent financial backers, William H. Vanderbilt and J. P. Morgan, who used the systems to light their palatial Manhattan mansions. Edison's isolated plants would, in fact, remain popular for many years to come.

As the spring of 1882 turned into summer, the many

components of the First District were finally coming together: the underground cable installations, the wiring of buildings, the installation of fixtures and meters, and the completion of the big dynamos that would power the system.

Inevitably, there were last-minute problems. In July, Edison scheduled a test of his new Jumbo generators at the Pearl Street station. Two of them had been linked together and were to be driven by a pair of powerful steam engines. "At first everything worked all right," Edison recalled. "Then we started another engine and threw them in parallel. Of all the circuses since Adam was born, we had the worst then! One engine would stop and the other would run up to a thousand revolutions; and then they would seesaw."

The entire building shook. Sparks flew. One observer described the scene as "terrifying." Edison grabbed the throttle of one engine, an associate grabbed the other, and together they shut down the machines. The problem was traced to a defect in the steam engines. Edison would later solve the problem by switching to a different type of steam engine, but for the time being, his embarrassment at the mishap made him much more secretive about testing the equipment.

On September 4, Edison was ready to begin operation of the Pearl Street station. Although the First District was not yet wired to its planned capacity of 33,000 lamps, some 800 lights in about 25 buildings, including the Drexel-Morgan Building and the offices of the *New York Times,* were waiting for Edison to throw the switch.

At 3:00 P.M. he did so. Describing the event, the *New York Herald* remarked on the "steady glare, bright and mellow, which illuminated interiors and shone through windows fixed and unwavering." Although many had doubted Edison, the newspaper said, "the test was fairly stood and the luminous horseshoes did their work well."

For his part, Edison delivered a simple pronouncement. "I have accomplished all I promised," he said.

CHAPTER

8

West Orange

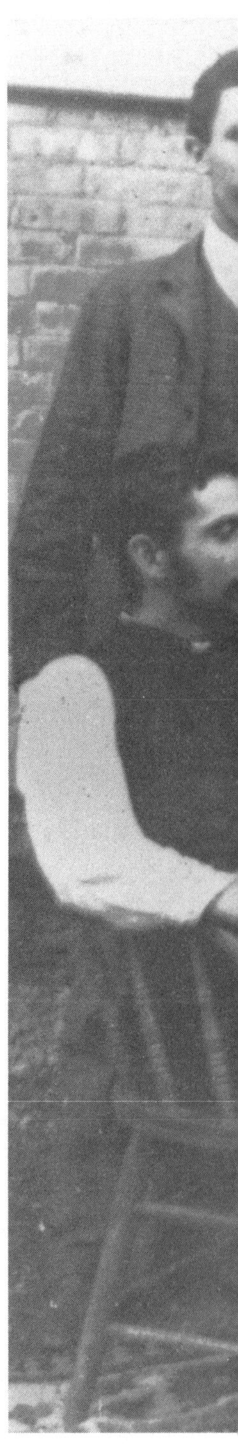

By the mid-1880s, Edison was both a millionaire and one of the best-known men alive. Still in his 30s, he had launched an industry that would, over the next several decades, spread its lights throughout the country and the world.

In the midst of this career triumph, arguably the greatest he would know, the inventor suffered personal tragedy. From 1882 to 1884, Mary Edison's health steadily deteriorated. She was plagued by severe headaches and often became irrational. On August 9, 1884, she died at Menlo Park. She was only 29 years old. Edison later told his daughter, Dot, that the cause of death was typhoid fever, but given Mary's symptoms it is more likely that she had a brain tumor.

Although the marriage had not been a happy one, Edison was deeply grieved by Mary's death. During the last two years of her life, despite the countless demands and responsibilities that came with the launching of the light-and-power system, he had tried to devote more time to her. After she died, he rarely returned to Menlo Park, and the famous laboratory fell into ruin.

This picture was taken in June 1888, after Edison and his workers had labored around the clock for three days while trying to improve the phonograph.

Edison now spent most of his time in New York, maintaining an apartment on 18th Street. His two boys, Thomas, Jr., and Will, were cared for mostly by Mary's mother, but Edison doted over Dot, who was now nearly 12. He took her to the theater, the opera, and Delmonico's, his favorite restaurant, often keeping her up well into the early morning hours.

In less than two years, Edison would remarry and return to New Jersey. Through an old friend, Edison met a young woman named Mina Miller in 1885. Her father, Lewis Miller of Akron, Ohio, was himself a wealthy inventor and manufacturer of farming implements. A 19-year-old black-haired beauty who was attending a Boston finishing school at the time Edison met her, Mina was smart, well-bred, and charming. Although Edison was twice her age, he fell in love with her from almost the moment they were introduced.

The courtship pleased Mina's father, who greatly admired Edison. Mina's mother, Mary, and her older sister, Jane, had some doubts, worrying that Mina might be rushing into things. Edison, self-confident and determined as always, pursued Mina without letup, and when he proposed during the late summer of 1885, she quickly accepted. Afterward, Mina fretted a bit over her decision—in part because it meant breaking off her engagement with another man, whose family had long been close to the Millers. Her doubts began to evaporate, however, as plans for the wedding developed.

The couple was wed in an elaborate ceremony at the Miller home on February 24, 1886. For their honeymoon, Edison took his new bride to Fort Myers, Florida, where he had recently purchased property and was building a winter home.

For a permanent residence, Edison might have chosen New York, where his business connections were centered. Mina, however, preferred a quieter environment. Before their marriage, they settled on West Orange, New Jersey, and for $250,000, Edison bought a grand, rambling mansion called Glenmont in the lavish residential neighborhood of Llewellyn Park.

Like Mary Edison, Mina would bear the inventor a daughter and two sons: Madeleine, born in 1888; Charles, born in 1890; and Theodore, born in 1898. And like Mary, Mina would discover that Thomas Edison was a persistent suitor but an inattentive husband. Work, she found, would always be his first priority. "He invents all the while, even in his dreams," she would observe.

And in 1886, there was much inventing still to be done. Edison was now planning the construction of a new laboratory more elaborate than any ever built. In January 1887, he purchased 14 acres of land in West Orange, about a half mile from his Glenmont estate. By early fall, five new buildings had been erected under Charles Batchelor's supervision.

The main laboratory, three stories high and containing nearly 40,000 square feet of floor space, included a beautiful wood-paneled library, offices, experiment rooms, a power house (containing dynamos, steam engines, and a boiler), machine shops, and storage space. The four smaller buildings housed laboratories devoted to electrical testing, chemical and metallurgical experiments, and woodworking.

Edison's new laboratory in West Orange, New Jersey, was much larger and more elaborate than the one he had maintained in Menlo Park.

Edison with his second wife, Mina, photographed shortly after their marriage in 1886.

Just as he had done at Menlo Park, Edison spared nothing to equip the lab. He installed the best available machines and instruments in the workshops and experiment rooms, filled the library with every book and scientific journal he could possibly need, and brought in supplies by the wagonload—tools, chemicals, mineral specimens, and just about every other kind of material. As Edison saw it, "the most important part of an experimental laboratory is a big scrap heap."

Employing about a hundred men, the West Orange laboratory was designed to pursue a wide range of projects. And in the decades ahead, Edison's work was nothing if not diversified.

Not surprisingly, electrical experiments made up much of the work done in the early years at West Orange. Improving the Edison system and its components—lamps, generators, metering devices, insulating materials—remained a top priority. The West Orange lab became the center for testing and developing the products being manufactured by the various Edison companies, such as the machine works and lamp factory.

Staying ahead of his rivals was a big concern for Edison, and the light-and-power industry he had created was now drawing heavy competition. One of those competitors was George Westinghouse, who in 1869 had patented an air brake for trains. After entering the electrical field in the mid-1880s, Westinghouse began promoting a power system that posed a major challenge to Edison's.

Westinghouse based his system on alternating current (AC) as opposed to the direct current (DC) used in Edison's system. In direct current, electricity flows in only one direction. In alternating current, the flow is reversed at regular intervals (60 times a second is today's AC standard). The main advantage of AC, and one that Westinghouse pushed heavily, is its suitability to high-voltage systems. (Voltage is the force, or pressure, with which electricity flows through a circuit.) And, as Westinghouse pointed out, having a high-voltage system would make the long-range distribution of electricity much cheaper and easier.

Edison mounted an intense campaign against AC, arguing that high-voltage systems were a public hazard. To demonstrate those dangers, he allowed an independent engineer named Harold P. Brown, another opponent of Westinghouse, to conduct a series of gruesome experiments in the West Orange dynamo room in 1888. Using an AC generator, Brown electrocuted a variety of animals—dogs, cats, a calf, and a horse—all to show that Westinghouse was promoting a deadly system.

Despite his fierce opposition to Westinghouse and a genuine concern for public safety, Edison did recognize the advantage of high-voltage systems. He conducted experiments of his own with both AC and a high-voltage DC system. Still, Edison never managed to produce a practical alternative to Westinghouse's system, and AC, in the end, became the industry standard.

During these years, Edison was actually losing much of the control he had earlier enjoyed over the electrical industry. In 1889, the financiers who backed him, notably Henry Villard and J. P. Morgan, consolidated the Edison Electric Light Company with the various Edison manufacturing companies, such as the lamp works and machine works, to form Edison General Electric. Three years later, Villard and Morgan merged the company with a smaller firm, the Thomson-Houston Company, creating General Electric (GE) and dropping Edison's name from that of the company altogether.

Edison continued to carry out electrical research for GE for several more years, although he was clearly unhappy with the turn of events. A member of the company's board of directors, he hardly ever attended its meetings, and he gradually sold off his GE stock to help finance other projects.

At about the same time that Edison's ties to the electric industry were weakening, he renewed his interest in the invention that had first established him in the public mind as a wizard—the phonograph. Edison had not touched the little talking machine in years because of his intense preoccupation with the problems of light and power. This neglect had allowed others to start tinkering with what Edison had always considered his most original invention.

In 1881, Alexander Graham Bell, the inventor of the telephone, had joined with his cousin, Chichester Bell, and another inventor, Charles Tainter, to make improvements in the phonograph. They replaced Edison's sheet of tinfoil with a more durable wax cylinder, and they improved the recording mechanism so that it worked more smoothly. To rotate the cylinder, they used a foot treadle instead of a hand crank. The Bell-Tainter machine was called (in a reversal of Edison's terminology) a graphophone. It was an altogether superior device, offering much better sound reproduction than Edison's original invention.

The Bells and Tainter applied for patents on the graphophone when Edison's patents lapsed in 1885. They set up their own company the following year and approached Edison with what they thought was a generous offer. They proposed joining forces with Edison to further improve the talking machine and offered to bear all the experimental and manufacturing costs.

Edison would have none of it. Considering the Bells and Tainter mere pirates, he vowed to create and manufacture an even better phonograph on his own. He quickly began work on an improved machine, and shortly after completing the West Orange laboratory, he established a phonograph factory nearby.

Edison's "perfected" phonograph borrowed heavily from the Bell-Tainter device but featured something that theirs did not: an electric motor. Edison had a prototype for a commercial machine ready by 1888, and his factory started producing the machines in the spring of 1889.

In the meantime, the rivalry between Edison and the Bell-Tainter group was settled when a businessman named Jesse Lippincott purchased both companies to form the North American Phonograph Company. Lippincott's main concern was with marketing the devices. The inventors each kept their own factories, with Edison manufacturing phonographs in West Orange and the Bell-Tainter group producing graphophones from its base in Washington, D.C.

Edison had long believed that the future of the phonograph lay in recording business dictation, and Lippincott was anxious that he develop the machine along those lines. But the early phonographs produced in West Orange turned out to be too delicate for strenuous office use and broke down easily. The wet-cell batteries that powered them were a nuisance to maintain, and the sound quality

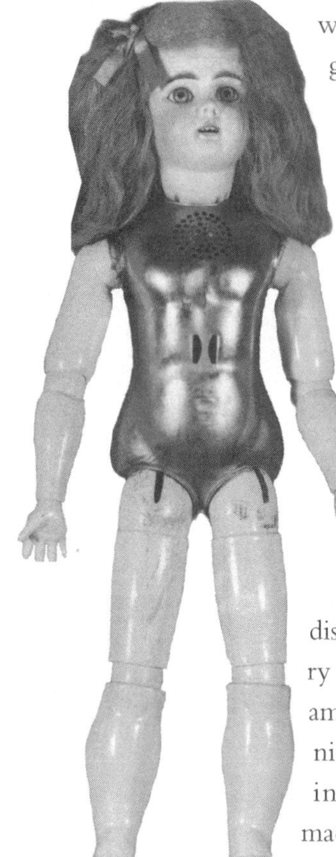

Edison used a miniature version of his phonograph to create this talking doll for children. Production of the dolls was stopped after only a year because of numerous technical problems.

was still poor. In this still primitive state, the phonograph would clearly not become part of the standard equipment in offices.

Edison also tried to use a miniature version of the phonograph to create a talking doll for children. This was another disaster. Placed inside the doll, the tiny spring-driven machine quickly failed, for the stylus simply would not stay within the groove of the prerecorded wax cylinder. Because of the technical problems, Edison stopped making the talking dolls late in 1890, only a year after production had begun.

Despite these setbacks, Edison found that the phonograph did have a future as an entertainment machine. There was a ready market, he discovered, for recorded music. The phonograph factory developed coin-operated machines for arcades, little amusement parlors where customers could enter, drop a nickel in a slot, and hear music through a special listening tube. The factory also turned out portable machines that traveling showmen could demonstrate at public gatherings. Edison started thinking as well about adapting the machine for home use and about finding a way to mass-produce recordings.

Even as Edison was discovering the entertainment potential of the phonograph, another project that would also revolutionize the world of entertainment was in development: motion pictures.

Edison had a long-standing interest in photography and included a photographic darkroom in the plan of the West Orange laboratory. One of the earliest visitors to the new lab was an Englishman named Eadweard Muybridge, a pioneering photographer who specialized in studies of people and animals in motion. Using multiple cameras, Muybridge had made thousands of sequential photographs that depicted horses galloping, birds flying, and humans engaging in a variety of activities, from walking to gymnastics.

Muybridge had mounted some of his photographs inside a device called a zoetrope, a rotating contraption that resembled a tiny carousel. By spinning the zoetrope and looking through the slots in its side, the viewer could see the appearance of movement. The illusion was due to a phenomenon known as persistence of vision, in which the brain retains an image an instant after it disappears. When passed before the eye in rapid succession, the series of still pictures seemed to flow together into a continuous action.

Muybridge's work fascinated Edison, who was soon pondering the possibility of producing a photographic device that would, as Edison explained it, "do for the eye what the phonograph does for the ear." In the inventor's original plan, the two inventions would be linked together

text continued on page 110

Workers at the West Orange laboratory assembling coin-operated phonographs.

MOTION PICTURES: THE KINETOGRAPH AND BEYOND

In its early stages, the motion picture apparatus developed by the Edison lab bore little resemblance to what would finally come into use. In his first experiments (conducted in 1888 and 1889), W. K. L. Dickson tried to model the motion-picture camera and viewing device after the phonograph. He used a rotating cylinder, or drum, both to photograph the action and display the pictures. The end result was a series of tiny photographs arranged in a helix around the cylinder—much like the continuous groove in Edison's cylindrical phonograph records.

Unfortunately, the pictures used in this device were tiny—no more than one-sixteenth of an inch across—which meant that they had to be viewed through a microscope lens. Also, because the pictures were mounted on a curved surface, their edges tended to be out of focus. Edison and Dickson quickly realized that motion pictures in this form had no commercial potential.

Fortunately, several manufacturers were developing a new type of photographic material that would solve the problem. It was essentially the kind of film we have today: long strips of flexible celluloid coated with a photographic emulsion. Edison saw one such type of film during the summer of 1889 when he journeyed to Paris to attend a major industrial exposition. Etienne Marey, a French physiologist who made photographic motion studies similar to the Muybridge experiments, showed Edison a filmstrip with perforated edges. These little holes would allow the sprockets in a special camera to grab the film and pull it through the shutter assembly. "I knew instantly that Marey had the right idea," Edison declared.

Edison and Dickson had strip film with perforated edges made to order, first by the Eastman Company of Rochester, New York, and later by the Blair Company of Boston. The film they used was 35 millimeters wide, the same standard that is used in commercial motion pictures today.

While it was rather crude and looked very different from today's motion-picture camera, the Edison kinetograph established the basic way that such devices work. The typical movie camera uses a motor (either elec-

The sprocket holes along the edges of motion-picture film allow it to be advanced mechanically through a camera or projector.

tric or spring driven) to pull the film from a feed reel through the lens-and-shutter assembly onto a take-up reel. As each "frame" is exposed, a special mechanism holds the film dead still for an instant before advancing it to the next frame. This stop-and-go motion is crucial to the camera's operation, for otherwise the photographic images would be blurred.

The motion-picture projector (which replaced the peep-hole machine that Edison called a kinetoscope) works much like the camera. It has feed and take-up reels for holding the developed film and a motor that uses sprockets to pull the film—in the same stop-and-go manner—through a shutter-and-lens assembly. Instead of taking pictures, however, the projector displays them. A high-intensity electric light mounted behind the shutter shines through the transparent film and the lens and projects the images onto a screen. Since the projector in a movie theater is positioned at some distance from the screen, the images the audience sees are enormous.

text continued from page 107

to create talking pictures. Edison turned the project over to a young assistant, W. K. L. Dickson, who had become the official photographer of the West Orange labs.

Late in 1889, Dickson and his boss had decided on the basic design of a motion picture camera, which they called a kinetograph (loosely meaning "motion recorder"). It depended on a long, continuous strip of film with perforated edges. Powered by an electric motor, the kinetograph utilized sprocket wheels that pulled the filmstrip through a lens-and-shutter assembly. The lens focused the image, while the shutter rapidly opened and closed to expose each frame. In this way the camera could record, on one piece of film, a continuous action in a series of small still photographs.

To display the motion pictures, Edison created a separate device called a kinetoscope. From the outside, it looked like a plain wooden cabinet with a peephole at the top. Inside were a battery-powered motor and an arrangement of sprocket wheels around which the film was looped. When the kinetoscope was running, the viewer could watch the motion-picture images through the peephole. It

Edison's strip kinetograph. Though it looks very different from today's movie cameras, it operated on the same principle.

was designed for entertainment arcades much like the coin-slot phonograph.

In 1893, a strange-looking wooden building, covered with black tar paper, was erected on the grounds of the West Orange complex between the lab buildings and the phonograph factory. Nicknamed the Black Maria, it was the world's first motion-picture studio. Inside, Edison's men made dozens of short films, ranging from boxing matches to vaudeville skits. To light its performance area, the Black Maria had a skylight in its roof, and the entire building could be rotated on a circular track to take advantage of the different positions of the sun over the course of a day. From these primitive beginnings the movie industry emerged.

Motion pictures would prove to be, in the years ahead, one of the more profitable ventures pursued by the West Orange laboratory. But a different project, in which Edison invested high hopes and millions of dollars, turned into a complete disaster. This enterprise, which could truly be called "Edison's folly," was an operation for mining and refining iron ore. Edison had first become interested in the mining of metals back at Menlo Park when he was trying to find sources of platinum for his electric light. At the same time, his work with dynamos had thoroughly familiarized him with magnetic fields. These two interests led him to the idea of using a powerful electromagnet to separate iron ore from crushed rock. Some preliminary experiments with a magnetic ore separator were encouraging, but Edison's attention had soon been diverted to perfecting his light-and-power system.

In 1888, with the completion of the West Orange lab, Edison renewed his interest in the ore experiments, and before long it became a full-scale venture. He believed that his ore separator could offer a profitable means of extracting iron from the low-grade ore that remained in abandoned mines, such as those located in New Jersey and Pennsylvania. A consultant whom Edison had hired suggested promoting

The world's first motion picture studio was built on the grounds of the West Orange complex in 1893. Nicknamed the Black Maria, it was a crude wooden structure covered with black tar paper.

the new technology to various mining companies. Edison, however, was much too excited by it to turn it over to others and so decided to go into the mining business for himself.

A pilot plant Edison established at Bechtelville, Pennsylvania, in 1889 produced some promising results and convinced the inventor that he could make a fortune from ore-milling. In 1890 he began construction of a massive second plant at Ogden, New Jersey. Completed the following year, the operation would obsess Edison for more than a decade. The Ogden plant employed huge steam shovels, rock crushers, and a "separation tower" where the iron was extracted. An ingenious system of conveyor belts carried the ore along through the various stages of refinement.

Ambitious though it was, the Ogden plant was plagued with problems. The equipment broke down frequently. The iron produced in the mill had a high phosphorus content, making it brittle. The 1890 discovery of rich iron deposits in Minnesota produced major competition for Edison—a situation that got worse when the economic depression of the mid-1890s reduced the price of the higher-grade midwestern ore. Yet Edison was so convinced that the operation would eventually pay off that he persisted in it well past the point when he should have gotten out. He halted work at the mill in 1895, returned to the venture in 1897, and finally closed it for good in 1900.

In the end, Edison spent more than $2 million of his own assets (including the GE stock he owned) on the ore-milling scheme; other investors had contributed over $1 million more. "Well, it's all gone," Edison said, reflecting on his losses, "but we had a hell of a good time spending it!"

Edison at work on an optics experiment in 1893.

CHAPTER 9

Into the 20th Century

The ore-milling fiasco might well have spelled the end of Edison's career, but the inventor's knack for doing many things at once kept him afloat. His mass-entertainment inventions, the phonograph and motion pictures, proved to be both popular and profitable from the mid-1890s through the early years of the 20th century.

After the death of Jesse Lippincott in 1891, Edison regained the distribution rights to the phonographs being produced at West Orange. He formed a new firm called the National Phonograph Company, which sold his products directly from the factory to dealers. In 1896, he announced production of a new wind-up phonograph to replace the troublesome electric model. At the beginning of the 1890s, phonograph sales had amounted to about $25,000 a year. By the end of the decade, annual sales swelled to $250,000, and the phonograph factory employed about a thousand workers.

Edison was now committed to developing the phonograph as an amusement machine. This meant producing not only phonographs but recordings as well. By 1901, Edison's lab had perfected a duplication process for the mass production of prerecorded cylinders. The recordings, which played for two minutes, ranged from vaudeville acts and dance-hall tunes to military marches and solos from Gilbert and Sullivan operettas. An opera fan, Edison saw a future in recordings of what he called "good music," but the short playing times and problems in recording large musical ensembles made this an impossibility for the time being.

By the turn of the century, Edison's phonograph was a huge success. His phonograph factory employed about a thousand workers and offered 25 different models for sale.

Inevitably, competitors challenged Edison. Soon the recording and phonograph industry was divided among three major companies: Edison's National Phonograph Company; the Columbia Phonograph Company, which had taken over manufacture of the Bell-Tainter graphophones; and the Victor Talking Machine Company. Both Columbia and Victor were making machines that played flat, disk-type records. Disks had two advantages over Edison's cylinders: longer playing times and ease of storage. Since Edison could claim better sound reproduction, he was slow to enter the disk market. But again, as in his crusade against alternating current, Edison was on the losing side of the battle. Near the end of 1909, he decided to produce a line of disks, but it would take another three years before they went on the market.

The use that Edison had first foreseen for the phonograph, as a device for recording office dictation, was also revived at West Orange, starting in 1905. Over several decades, the once bug-laden machines were steadily made

An employee of Edison Phonographs makes a house call to deliver records and phonographs, around 1906.

sturdier, more compact, and easier to use. As they gained wider acceptance from businesses, Edison's dictating machines, along with those of his competitors, became as commonplace in offices as typewriters.

For years, phonograph production remained the largest of Edison's diverse enterprises, and National Phonograph became the core company when those enterprises were reorganized in 1910 under the name of Thomas A. Edison, Incorporated. The phonograph bore out the prophecy Edison had pronounced when he invented it. His "baby" did indeed "grow up and be a big feller" that helped to support the inventor in his old age.

Although Edison devoted fewer years to the motion picture business, for a while it too was a lively concern. Kinetoscope parlors flourished in the mid-1890s but declined quickly when projected films were introduced. In 1895 in faraway France, two brothers named Louis and Auguste Lumière developed a motion-picture camera that doubled as a projector, and before long other inventors were offering projectors as well. In 1896, production started at West Orange on a projector called the Edison vitascope. Despite its name, the projector was actually the creation of Thomas Armat, a young inventor who had reached an agreement with Edison for the manufacturing and marketing rights.

Competition in motion pictures came from such fledgling companies as Biograph, to which W. K. L. Dickson had defected in 1895. Through the turn of the century into the early 1900s, New Jersey and New York formed the center of a thriving movie industry, and theaters showing its products sprang up around the country. To keep up with his rivals, Edison spent $100,000 to build a new studio in the Bronx, a borough of New York City, in 1905. Three years later, the Motion Picture Patents Company was formed, linking Edison, Biograph, and eight other companies in a monopoly that for nearly 10 years controlled the production, distribution, and exhibition of all motion pictures made in the United States.

During these years, the subject matter of films gradually evolved from pictures of anything that moved to films that told stories. One of the earliest such movies was a 1903 Edison production called *The Great Train Robbery,* directed by Edwin S. Porter. Set in the Wild West (but filmed in New Jersey), it depicted the daring escapades of an outlaw band and ended with a close-up of a desperado aiming and shooting directly at the camera—a startling image that sent some audience members diving under their seats. The film was about 10 minutes long and excited the public's taste for more story films.

As movie fever swept the country, Edison's men struggled to find a way to synchronize recorded sound with motion pictures, but the problems finally proved too much even for a lab as well equipped as Edison's. Although Edison unveiled an early "talkie" system called a kinetophone at a New York vaudeville theater in 1913, the equipment was too complicated to gain widespread use. The kinetophone

The Great Train Robbery (1903) was one of the first movies that told a story. Only 10 minutes long, the film ended with this image of an outlaw aiming and shooting his gun directly at the audience.

quietly died. Talkies would not grace the nation's movie theaters until the late 1920s.

In 1918, Edison left the movie business altogether. Meanwhile, the center of the film industry had shifted from the East Coast to the sunnier climates of Southern California, where the name Hollywood quickly became synonymous with the movies.

In addition to the development of motion pictures and the phonograph, the work at West Orange included a dizzying array of other research. At one time or another, there were experiments with X rays, electric-train motors, flying machines, cheap housing made from poured concrete, and electric automobiles. These projects show the diversity of Edison's interests and the amazing fertility of his mind, even though many of them did not get very far.

Though experimental failures never dampened Edison's enthusiasm for invention, neither did setbacks of another kind. When fire destroyed much of the West Orange complex in December 1914 (though it spared the main laboratory), Edison scarcely blinked. Looking on as the spectacular flames consumed his factory buildings, Edison turned to his son Charles and said: "Where's Mother? Get her over here, and her friends too. They'll never see a fire like this again." Within days, he was rebuilding.

Edison's relentless determination was especially apparent in his efforts to develop an improved storage battery. (Storage batteries, unlike so-called primary batteries, can be periodically recharged.) In the late 1800s, lead-acid batteries were the only kind of storage battery in use; they depended on a chemical reaction involving lead, lead peroxide, and a sulfuric acid solution to produce the electric current. Edison believed that a better storage battery—something lighter, longer lasting, and more efficient than the lead-acid type—was possible, and throughout the early 1900s, his laboratory struggled to produce one. By 1909, after many a costly and frustrating experiment, a battery based on a reaction between nickel oxide, iron, and a potassium hydroxide solution was perfected. It found a variety of uses—in devices such as miner's lamps, train lights, and railroad signals—and became one of Edison's best-selling products. However, the main use Edison had originally intended for it, to power electric cars, faded when gasoline-powered automobiles, such as those produced by Henry Ford, came to dominate the growing car market between 1908 and 1910.

Edison's hopes for the battery brightened in 1912 when Ford asked him to adapt the battery to a car ignition system. Ford was looking for a better way to start his Model T than the familiar, arm-wrenching hand crank. Unfortunately, Edison's battery lacked sufficient power to start the motor and failed entirely in cold weather. But even though Edison's battery did not suit Ford's purposes, the inventor and the auto maker became good friends and later took vacation trips together.

Edison takes a ride in a car powered by one of his electric storage batteries.

Edison's storage battery also attracted the attention of the United States Navy, which was especially interested in using it to power its submarines. This interest intensified when World War I erupted among the European nations in 1914 and threatened to involve the United States as well. The navy not only tested Edison's batteries on its new experimental submarine, the E2, but in 1915 made the inventor chairman of the Naval Consulting Board.

Unfortunately, the E2 experiments had a tragic outcome. In 1916, hydrogen gas escaping from the batteries ignited, causing an explosion that killed five sailors. Although it was clear that the crew had ignored basic safety precautions, the batteries were blamed for the mishap. Any hopes Edison had for producing submarine batteries ended right there.

Despite the accident, Edison remained an active advisor to the navy and was instrumental in planning a naval research laboratory, which he modeled after the facility at West Orange. After the United States entered the war in 1917, he concentrated his experimental efforts on ways of detecting enemy submarines. The experiments produced no practical results, however, and the navy was not interested in any of Edison's other ideas. By the time the war ended in 1918, the inventor was disillusioned with the naval bureaucracy.

Edison expressed his keen disappointment in a letter to the secretary of the navy, Josephus Daniels, writing, "I do not believe there is one creative mind produced at Annapolis in three years. When you are no longer Secretary I want to tell you a lot of things about the Navy that you are unaware of."

During the first two decades of the 20th century, the West Orange complex grew into a major industrial operation. In 1900, Edison's factories employed about 3,000 workers; by 1920, more than 10,000 employees staffed his assembly lines. The laboratory, which formed what today would be called a research and development department, became only a tiny (if still vital) part of the total organization.

Edison throws out the first pitch at an employee baseball game in the 1920s.

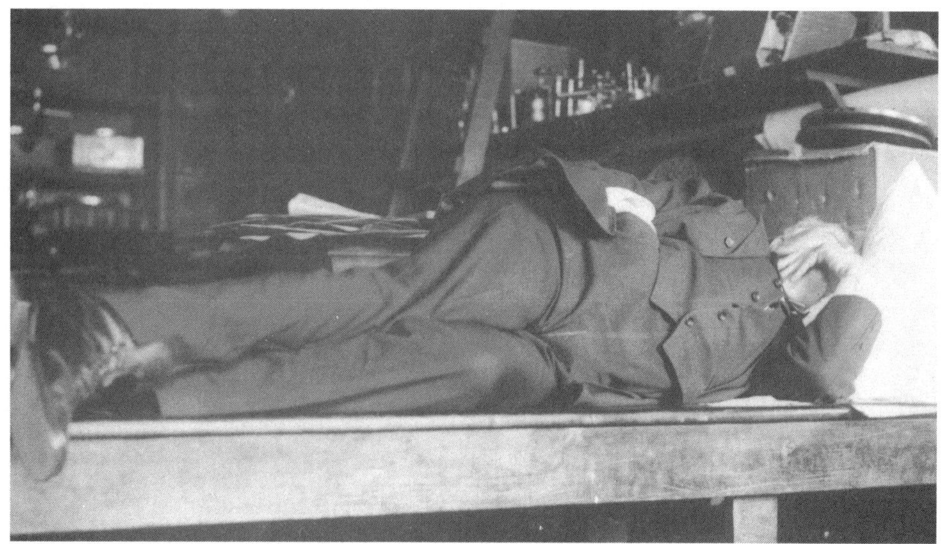

Edison asleep on a desk at his West Orange laboratory, 1911.

In running this industrial empire, Edison was not always the most progressive of bosses. With some of his men—especially those who had been with him a long time—he could be generous and would keep them on the payroll even after they stopped being productive. Yet, with most employees—the younger, college-trained researchers as well as the countless workers who assembled his phonographs, storage batteries, and other products—he was tough and uncompromising. He kept wages low—a lab chemist might make as little as $20 a week, while a factory worker as little as $1.50 a day. Long opposed to unions, he had little sympathy for the grievances of labor. When a strike occurred in 1903, for example, he had wasted no time in breaking it. As someone to whom work meant everything, Edison had trouble understanding why others could not be as dedicated to their jobs as he was.

Despite his advancing age, Edison refused to slow down. He even had a lab built at his winter home in Fort Myers, Florida, so that he could work during the months when he was away from West Orange.

Among the last projects in which the inventor was personally involved was an effort to find a domestic source of rubber. Because of World War I and the disruptions it caused in international trade, American businessmen realized the dangers of relying on foreign sources of raw materials. After the war ended, fears abounded that British and Dutch interests were conspiring to monopolize the rubber supply. These concerns prompted Edison, with financial help from Henry Ford and the tire maker Harvey Firestone, to begin an intensive search in the late 1920s for a homegrown plant that would yield a good supply of rubber.

Edison planted hundreds of shrubs and trees around his home in Fort Myers and enlisted the aid of dozens of botanists, both professionals and amateurs, in collecting plant specimens. His obsession with the project, which was typical of how he approached everything he ever did, caused Mina to note: "Everything has turned to rubber in our family. We talk rubber, think rubber, dream rubber."

Edison continued working on the rubber project right up to the eve of his death and did manage to produce a high strain of rubber from the goldenrod plant. By this time, however, the British and Dutch attempts at monopoly had collapsed. Rubber prices dropped, and the fears about a short supply faded. Yet, although the project had little impact in the end, it kept Edison busy and happy. He had officially retired in 1926, leaving the administration of his company to his son Charles. Searching for rubber gave him an ongoing sense of purpose.

By this time, however, his health was starting to fail. Given the fact that he had never eaten properly in his life—pie and coffee were the mainstays of his diet—and that he smoked cigars and chewed tobacco regularly, it is amazing that he lived into his 80s. But his bad habits and his advancing age were finally taking their toll. Diabetes, kidney problems, and an ulcer were among the problems that tormented him during these final years.

In October 1929, Edison was barely able to get through a grand celebration, called Light's Golden Jubilee, that was

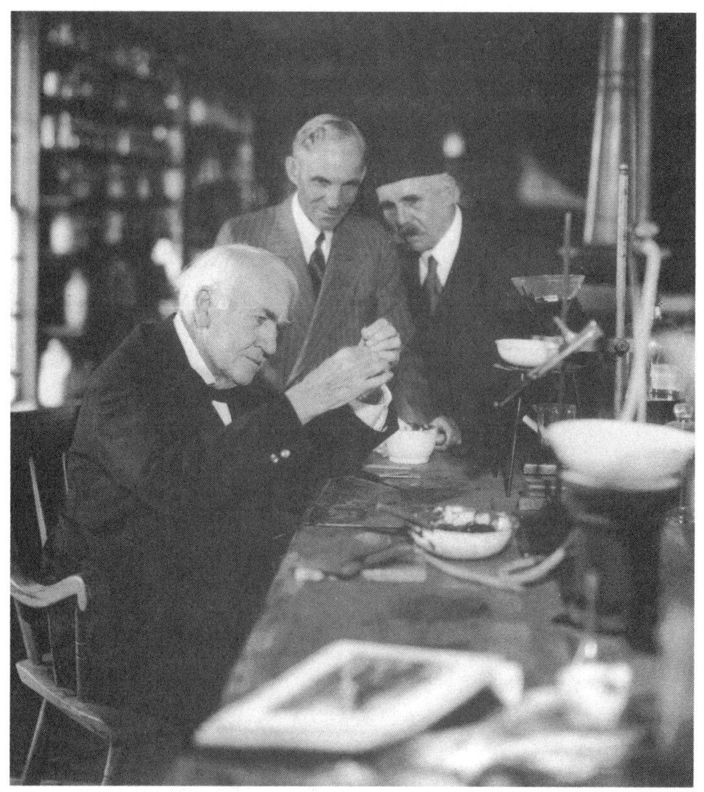

To mark the 50th anniversary of the electric light in 1929, auto maker Henry Ford built a reconstruction of Edison's Menlo Park lab at Greenfield Village, a collection of historic buildings in Dearborn, Michigan. With Ford (center) and Edison's old assistant, Francis Jehl, looking on, Edison re-enacts the making of the electric lamp.

arranged in his honor. In Dearborn, Michigan, his friend Henry Ford combined this commemoration of the incandescent light's 50th anniversary with the opening of a pair of the auto maker's pet projects. One was a museum that showcased the products of American invention and industry. The other was a collection of historic buildings that included a replica of the Menlo Park laboratory. Among its other reproductions were the boarding house where the Menlo Park staff had stayed and the railroad car where young Alva Edison had installed one of his first laboratories.

Frail as he was, Edison enjoyed the proceedings and was especially delighted with the reconstruction of the lab. He had one criticism of its authenticity, however. "We never kept it as clean as this!" he told Ford.

The climax of the festivities was Edison's lighting of a carbon-filament lamp, a replica of the one he and his men had devised back in Menlo Park. "Will it light? Will it burn?" a radio announcer asked breathlessly. Then, a moment later, the announcer trumpeted: "Ladies and gentlemen—it lights! Light's Golden Jubilee has come to a triumphant climax!"

Though he was so weak he was near collapse, Edison managed to read a short speech in which he noted that "in honoring me you are also honoring that vast army of thinkers and workers without whom my work would have gone for nothing." President Herbert Hoover delivered the concluding speech. But Edison heard none of it. Worn out, he had allowed Mina and his doctor to take him to another room.

Although Edison kept working on the rubber project for the next two years, his health continued to decline. Rarely visiting the laboratory, he spent most of his time at Glenmont or in Fort Myers. Finally, as the fall of 1931 came and the New Jersey leaves changed color, it became clear to Mina and the rest of the family that the great inventor was near death. Confined to bed, unable to eat, he soon reached the same conclusion himself. For probably the first time ever, Thomas Alva Edison simply gave up.

He slipped into a coma on October 14. During the early hours of October 18, he died. He was 84 years old.

The world mourned his passing. Thousands came to West Orange to view his body as it lay in state in the laboratory library. On October 21, the day of his funeral at Glenmont, President Hoover proposed a fitting tribute: at 10 P.M., as many lights as possible were to be dimmed around the country.

The countless contributions of Edison and his associates—the quadruplex telegraph, the phonograph, the practical incandescent light, the electrical distribution system, the crucial improvements in the telephone and electrical generators, the motion picture camera—made Edison a liv-

A dapper Thomas Edison sits on the grounds of his estate, Glenmont, in June, 1917.

ing legend and have been justly celebrated time and again in the years since his death.

But just as worthy as these inventions, though perhaps not as well remembered, were Edison's pioneering efforts in creating an industrial research laboratory, first at Menlo Park and then at West Orange. The Edison-style lab, which joined financial resources, the best equipment, and talented personnel in an organized quest for new products and innovations, became the model for other companies. When Edison died, more than 1,500 industrial research laboratories were in operation. Today such labs continue to be the source of what is popularly called "high tech." Edison was thus a key transitional figure who bridged the gap between the crude workshops of the 19th century and the gleaming facilities that make up the research and development departments within modern corporations.

The most famous saying attributed to Edison—that genius is "one percent inspiration and ninety-nine percent perspiration"—summed up the inventor's lifelong belief in doggedly working through the problems of any given project. Yet the statement underestimates the role of inspiration in Thomas Edison's work. That special creative spark, the ability to conceive of things no one else has thought of, was definitely present in Edison, and it was a critical factor in his success.

Closely linked to Edison's creative gifts were his unfailing optimism and extraordinary confidence in himself. That confidence, which included a flair for brash showmanship and which often surfaced as unrestrained boastfulness, helped Edison over many a rough spot. It kept him going in the face of experimental setbacks and competition from rivals, and it reassured conservative investors who might otherwise have withdrawn their support.

In the end, probably no one can say exactly why Edison so towered above all other inventors. But the world can only be grateful that he did.

1847
Born Thomas Alva Edison in Milan, Ohio, on February 11

1854
Family moves to Port Huron, Michigan

1859
Works as candy butcher on Grand Trunk Railroad

1863
Works as itinerant telegrapher

1868
Takes job in Western Union office in Boston, Massachusetts

1869
Quits Western Union to become freelance inventor; receives first patent for electric vote recorder; moves to New York City; forms a "General Telegraphic Agency" with Frank Pope and James Ashley

1870
Forms partnership with William Unger in Newark, New Jersey, to make stock printers for Gold & Stock; begins work for Automatic Telegraph Company

1871
Marries Mary Stilwell

1874
Invents quadruplex telegraph

1875
Becomes involved in legal dispute over ownership of quadruplex

1876
Moves to Menlo Park, New Jersey, and establishes laboratory

1877
Invents the carbon-button telephone transmitter and the phonograph

1879
Invents a practical incandescent lamp

1880
Perfects a system of electrical distribution

1881
Moves bulk of operations to New York City and begins installation of an electrical distribution system

1882
Pearl Street central lighting station in New York begins operation

1884
Death of Mary Edison

1886
Marries Mina Miller; moves to West Orange, New Jersey

1887
Completes new laboratory complex in West Orange; resumes work on phonograph

1888
Begins ore-milling experiments; mounts campaign against alternating current promoted by George Westinghouse

1889
Begins development of motion picture devices—the kinetograph and kinetoscope—and starts production of improved phonograph; Edison General Electric formed

In 1886, Edison purchased Glenmont, a 29-room mansion, located in West Orange, New Jersey.

1890
Constructs ore-milling plant in Ogden, New Jersey

1892
General Electric formed; Edison's ties to electric industry start to weaken

1893
First movie studio—the Black Maria—built at West Orange

1894
Forms National Phonograph Company

1896
Introduces a new spring-motor phonograph

1900
Closes ore-milling plant

1903
The Great Train Robbery released

A man peers into Edison's kinetoscope in 1895.

1905

Reintroduces a dictating machine

1908

Motion Picture Patents Company formed

1909

Perfects a practical nickel-iron storage battery

1910

Reorganizes his companies as Thomas A. Edison, Inc.

1912

Tries to develop auto ignition system for Henry Ford

1914
Fire destroys portion of West Orange complex

1915
Named chairman of Naval Consulting Board

1918
Ends involvement in motion pictures

1926
Retires as head of Thomas A. Edison, Inc.

1927
Undertakes search for domestic source of rubber

1929
Light's Golden Jubilee held in Dearborn, Michigan

1931
Thomas Edison dies at home in West Orange, New Jersey, on October 18

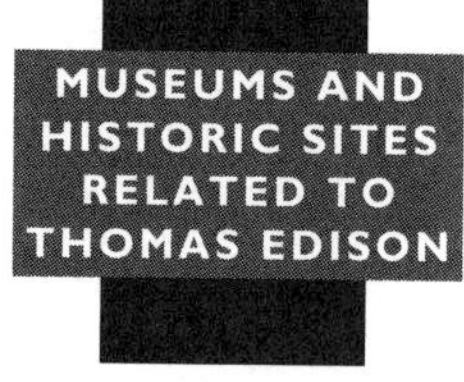

Edison National Historic Site

Main Street and Lakeside Avenue
West Orange, NJ 07052
Tel. 201-736-5050 (recorded information and directions)
Tel. 201-736-0550 (group information and reservations)

The National Park Service now preserves Edison's research laboratory much as it was in the inventor's day. The archive housing Edison's enormous collection of papers and records is maintained here. Visitors can see the library, machine shop, chemical lab, a replica of the Black Maria movie studio, and demonstrations of the early phonograph. Glenmont, the nearby Edison estate, is also open for tours. The house contains the original furnishings used by Thomas and Mina Edison, who are buried on the grounds.

Edison Winter Home

2350 McGregor Boulevard
Fort Myers, FL 33901
Tel. 813-334-3614

Willed to the city of Fort Myers by Mina Edison, the 14-acre Edison winter estate includes a botanical garden where the inventor cultivated various plants used in his research, such as bamboo for lamp filaments and goldenrod for rubber production. Among the buildings are the main house, a honeymoon cottage, a chemical laboratory, and a museum, completed in 1970, which exhibits an impressive array of Edison inventions. The winter home of Edison's close friend Henry Ford is also located in Fort Myers.

Edison Birthplace Museum

9 Edison Drive
Milan, OH 44846
Tel. 419-499-2135

Overlooking what remains of the historic Milan canal basin, the house where Edison was born is now maintained as a museum. It features furniture from the period, as well as family memorabilia. It also contains an exhibit of Edison's inventions, among them a model of the original phonograph and an early electric light bulb.

Henry Ford Museum and Greenfield Village

20900 Oakwood Boulevard
Dearborn, MI 48121
Tel. 313-271-1620

This complex was the scene of "Light's Golden Jubilee" in 1929. Greenfield Village includes reconstructions of the Menlo Park laboratory and the nearby boarding house where Edison's staff stayed, as well as many other historic buildings, such as Orville Wright's bicycle shop and a courthouse where Abraham Lincoln once practiced law. The museum, a celebration of industry and technology, exhibits everything from farm implements to automobiles to household items, including devices that originated with Edison.

Museum of Arts and History

1115 6th Street
Port Huron, MI 48060
Tel. 313-982-0891

While Edison's boyhood home in Port Huron no longer stands, artifacts taken from an archaeological investigation of the site are on display at this museum.

Menlo Park Memorial Tower

Route 27
Edison, NJ 08817
Tel. 201-549-3299

A 131-foot-high tower, topped with a 14-foot-high light bulb, commemorates the site of Edison's Menlo Park laboratory.

Con-Edison Energy Museum

145 East 14th Street
New York, NY 10011
Tel. 212-460-6244

Exhibits on early electric lighting are among the attractions at this museum, run by the New York City power company that still bears Edison's name.

Schenectady Museum and Planetarium

Knot Terrace Heights
Schenectady, NY 12305
Tel. 518-382-7890

This museum includes exhibits of early General Electric products.

Thomas Edison Butchertown House

729 East Washington
Louisville, KY 40202
Tel. 502-583-8317

The young Edison stayed at this cottage during one of his stints as a telegrapher in Louisville. Edison memorabilia and inventions—including a phonograph, cylinder records, and early light bulbs—are among the displays.

Biographies and General Works on Edison

Baldwin, Neil. *Edison: Inventing the Century*. New York: Hyperion, 1995.

Buranelli, Vincent. *Thomas Alva Edison*. Englewood Cliffs, N.J.: Silver Burdett, 1989.

Clark, Ronald W. *Edison: The Man Who Made the Future*. New York: Putnam, 1977.

Conot, Robert. *A Streak of Luck*. New York: Seaview Books, 1979. Reprint, New York: Da Capo, 1986.

Josephson, Matthew. *Edison: A Biography*. New York: McGraw-Hill, 1959. Reprint, New York: John Wiley, 1992.

Millard, Andre. *Edison and the Business of Innovation*. Baltimore: Johns Hopkins University Press, 1990.

Vanderbilt, Byron M. *Thomas Edison, Chemist*. Washington, D.C.: American Chemical Society, 1971.

Wachhorst, Wyn. *Thomas Alva Edison: An American Myth*. Cambridge, Mass.: MIT Press, 1981.

Working at Inventing: Thomas A. Edison and the Menlo Park Experience. Introduction by William A. Pretzer. Dearborn, Mich.: Henry Ford Museum, 1989.

The Papers of Thomas Edison

Edison, Thomas A. *The Papers of Thomas A. Edison, Volume 1: The Making of an Inventor, February 1847–June 1873*. Edited by Reese V. Jenkins, et. al. Baltimore: Johns Hopkins University Press, 1989.

———. *The Papers of Thomas A. Edison, Volume 2: From Workshop to Laboratory, June 1873–March 1876*. Edited by Robert A. Rosenberg, et al. Baltimore: Johns Hopkins University Press, 1992.

———. *The Papers of Thomas A. Edison, Volume 3: Menlo Park, The Early Years, April 1876–December 1877*. Edited by Robert A. Rosenberg, et al. Baltimore: Johns Hopkins University Press, 1994.

On Inventing and Inventors

Flatow, Ira. *They all Laughed...From Light Bulbs to Lasers, the Fascinating Stories Behind the Great Inventions That Have Changed Our Lives.* New York: HarperCollins, 1992.

Noonan, Geoffrey, J. *Nineteenth-Century Inventors.* New York: Facts on File, 1991.

Weaver, Rebecca and Rodney Dale. *Home Entertainment.* New York: Oxford University Press, 1993.

Williams, Trevor I. *The History of Invention: From Stone Axes to Silicon Chips.* New York: Facts on File, 1987.

Motion Pictures

Musser, Charles. *Thomas A. Edison and His Kinetographic Motion Pictures.* West Orange, N.J.: Friends of Edison National Historic Site, 1993. Reprint, New Brunswick, N.J.: Rutgers University Press, 1995.

Robinson, David. *From Peep Show to Palace: The Birth of American Film.* New York: Columbia University Press, 1995.

The Phonograph

Gelatt, Roland. *The Fabulous Phonograph, 1877–1977.* New York: Macmillan, 1977.

Welch, Walter L. and Leah Stenzel Burt. *From Tinfoil to Stereo: The Acoustic Years of the Recording Industry.* Gainesville: University Press of Florida, 1994.

Electricity and the Electric Light

Boltz, C. L. *How Electricity Is Made.* New York: Facts on File, 1985.

Friedel, Robert, and Paul Israel, with Bernard S. Finn. *Edison's Electric Light: Biography of an Invention.* New Brunswick, N.J.: Rutgers University Press, 1986.

Sharlin, Harold I. *The Making of the Electrical Age: From the Telegraph to Automation.* New York: Abelard-Schuman, 1963.

Silverberg, Robert. *Light for the World: Edison and the Power Industry.* Princeton, N.J.: D. Van Nostrand Company, 1967.

Page numbers in *italics* indicate illustrations.

ACKNOWLEDGMENTS

Like generations of Americans before me, I became fascinated by Thomas Edison's achievements at an early age. I still recall devouring the encyclopedia entries about his life and inventions and watching avidly whenever the old MGM movies—*Young Tom Edison* with Mickey Rooney and *Edison the Man* with Spencer Tracy—appeared on television. Some of that boyish enthusiasm returned in the late 1970s when, as one of several graduate students enrolled in Miles Kreuger's class in film research methods at Columbia University, I visited the Edison National Historic Site in West Orange, New Jersey; there, as Mr. Kreuger aptly put it, "you can feel Edison's presence everywhere." So, in 1992, when Nancy Toff of Oxford University Press suggested that I write on Edison as part of the Oxford Portraits in Science series, I felt not a moment's hesitation about climbing aboard. For initiating this project, Nancy deserves special thanks.

I am grateful as well to Paul McCarthy, project editor at Oxford, who has been wonderfully helpful in guiding this book toward publication. He showed admirable patience throughout the process and especially with my penchant for making last-minute changes in page proof. David Carter, the copyeditor, offered countless valuable suggestions for improving the manuscript.

Professor Mark C. Miller of Clark University helped me clear up a point of confusion about the response to Edison's vote recorder, and Karen Sloat-Olsen of the Edison National Historic Site provided useful information not only about that fascinating place but about other Edison-related sites around the country. Jim and Donna Kelly came up with additional material relating to the Edison winter home in Fort Myers, Florida, along with a complete list of Edison's patents.

My parents, Irma Lee Adair and the late Robert W. Adair, will always have my gratitude for their lifelong support, which includes, not least, encouraging me in an early love of books. My wife, Leslie K. Adair, has been enormously supportive—and patient—during the writing and editing phases of this project.

Of course, any defects and errors that remain in this work are my responsibility alone.

American Institute of Physics Emilio Segrè Visual Archives, E. Scott Barr Collection: 37; Diagram by Gary Tong: 28; U.S. Department of the Interior, National Park Service, Edison National Historic Site: cover, frontispiece, 8, 10, 12, 15, 16, 19, 22, 24, 30, 32, 38, 41, 44, 48, 49, 52, 55, 56, 59, 61, 65, 66, 72, 74, 79, 82, 84, 87, 90, 94, 98, 101, 102, 106, 107, 109, 110, 112, 114, 116, 117, 119, 121, 122, 123, 125, 127, 131, 132.

Gene Adair, who has worked in publishing since 1981, is currently the marketing manager at the University of Tennessee Press. A former teacher and newspaper reporter, he is also the author of a young adult biography of George Washington Carver. He holds a Master of Fine Arts degree in film studies from Columbia University.

Owen Gingerich is a senior astronomer at the Smithsonian Astrophysical Observatory and Professor of Astronomy and of the History of Science at Harvard University. He has served as vice president of the American Philosophical Society and as chairman of the U.S. National Committee of the International Astronomical Union. The author of more than 400 articles and reviews, Professor Gingerich is also the author of *The Great Copernicus Chase and Other Adventures in Astronomical History,* and *The Eye of Heaven: Ptolemy, Copernicus, Kepler.* The International Astronomical Union's Minor Planet Bureau has named Asteroid 2658 "Gingerich" in his honor.